Living a Rich Life

Living a Rich Life

Achieving Personal,
Financial and Spiritual
Abundance
Following Mary Kay's
Laws of Living Rich

WRITTEN BY

Sharon Morgan Tahaney

MARY KAY INC.

16251 Dallas Parkway

Dallas, TX 75248

www.marykay.com

Design by Anne Winslow.

Printed in the United States of America.

Published by Forbes Custom Publishing Inc., New York City.

ACKNOWLEDGMENTS

What an incredible example of collaboration! This book grew from the minds and hearts of so many. I would first like to thank Mary Kay Ash, whose immense courage, determination and vision drew us all together making this book possible. Her wisdom illuminates every page and I will forever be grateful for the privilege of learning about life and business from her tutelage.

My thanks also go to the many Mary Kay Independent Sales Directors who so openly shared their stories of wins and losses and everything in between during the course of living and learning as women, wives, mothers and entrepreneurs. Their lessons add depth and color to the knowledge this book passes on to others.

I would also like to thank the Sales Directors who defined "living rich" for us throughout the book. Their definitions framed this book beautifully and I thank them for opening their hearts and dreams to us all.

My gratitude also goes to Mary Kay management, who believed it our duty to put feet on Mary Kay's mission by delivering to women a book that lived and breathed the truth of spiritual, personal and financial abundance.

I also owe much appreciation to the editors at Forbes. I have been genuinely impressed by the professionalism, high standards, diligence and gracious working style of Katie Calhoun and Barbara Strauch. It's been a pleasure and a sense of comfort to partner with this dedicated and competent Forbes team.

I'm also indebted to the wisdom and experience of authors who came before me—specifically Edward de Bono, Gary Belsky, Thomas Gilovich, Nicholas G. Apostolou, D. Larry Crumbley and Bill Griffeth. I drew on their knowledge which added immensely to the usefulness of this book.

And a special thanks goes to the Mary Kay staff who edited, refined and directed this book every step of the way. I owe much to their razor-sharp accuracy in detail and correctness, their knowledge of the sales force, their keen sense of organization and their tireless efforts in refining the manuscript with efficiency and calm professionalism. Their hearts beat with the love and character of Mary Kay Ash and, combined with the hundreds of thousands of Mary Kay Sales Directors and Beauty Consultants, create a family of businesswomen I am honored to be a part of. Thank you all! ❧

FOREWORD

WHEN MARY KAY ASH ESTABLISHED HER COMPANY in 1963, she was the product of a business world that not only excluded women but too often set roadblocks in their paths. She was determined to change that. She succeeded beyond even her fondest hopes.

Despite nearly four decades of success, we who are guardians of her dream do not intend to rest on our laurels. Our opportunity today is to seek new and meaningful ways to inspire women to believe in themselves. One of the most important is to help women find balance in all areas of their lives. This book takes a woman's look at financial truths. It is based on real life successes and stories related by members of the Mary Kay Independent Sales Force.

Mary Kay continues to open doors to success. When we talk about "enrichment," we are speaking not only of monetary rewards, but also of making good on Mary Kay's dream of enriching all aspects of a woman's life, including those which can never be measured in dollars.

Those of us who have had the privilege to know Mary Kay Ash understand why it is so important that we produce such a book.

As Mary Kay has said on many occasions, "This Company is about so much more than selling lipstick."

Our independent sales force enlightens us with four generations of real-life examples. We are privileged to have learned a great deal from these wonderful stories. When we put all of our experience together, the result is a powerful arsenal of knowledge that can have far-reaching benefits to families everywhere seeking to live a rich life.

—JOHN P. ROCHON
Chairman

Living a Rich Life

RICH. THE MEANING OF THAT WORD first formed in your mind when that kid in class got the new bike for Christmas—the bright red Schwinn with the banana seat, silver chrome basket and vanity license on the back bumper. "She must be *rich* to get a bike like that," you thought. Or maybe it was the Barbie and Ken dolls or the leather-trimmed winter coat or the shiny, new pair of roller skates that formed your definition of "rich." Whatever the thing that gave meaning to "rich," the point is . . . it was probably a "thing."

That was then. You and I both know that times have changed. We're all grown up now, and, fortunately, "rich" has grown up too. It's not about things anymore. It's not about looking the part. It's not about keeping up with the Joneses or one-upping the neighbor. In fact, it's not about anything we own or wear or drive or count. It's about *being*. Not *seeming* to be. *Being*. Being more alive. Being more secure. Being soulfully content. It's about being grounded in meaningful principles. It's about contributing to family and society. It's about doing what we came here to do and leaving a legacy after we're gone. Now *that's* living rich.

Exactly what Mary Kay Ash wants for you . . . has always wanted for you. Not simply to get by, but to live rich. This Company is her way of providing you the means. The purpose of this book is to help provide the motivation.

In our grown-up world, we've watched everything around us change. We've seen tax laws shift, markets fluctuate, interest rates go up and down with every sneeze of our chairman of the Federal Reserve. We've seen our nation confused—violence in our public buildings, in our schools and even in the very sanctuary of God. But remaining constant in all the turmoil are irrefutable natural laws, universal truths that are Biblical in origin and so familiar to us in Mary Kay. Our nation's founding fathers knew these laws. Thirty-four percent of all the quotes gathered from letters and documents created by them came from the Bible. They had it right then . . . Mary Kay has it right now. Her principles are pure. Her principles are positive. And if we apply this wisdom in all the tiny choices we make, minute by minute, of every day, our lives will be in sync, our finances in order. And the bonus? A rush of energy, a turning up the juice, a firing of passion and purpose—very simply, a rich life the Mary Kay way.

So before you jump into reading, let's take a quick overview of how this book evolved and what you can expect. First, when determining the voice for this book, I felt I should talk to you as if we were sitting together, having a chat. I, like you, am a focused and devoted student of Mary Kay Ash. I feel as W. B. Yeats did when he said, "If what I say resonates with you, it's merely because we are both branches on the same tree." That tree, of course, is Mary Kay. I have written for Mary Kay Inc. since 1982 and have absorbed into my life and into my family the principles and philosophies of Mary Kay Ash. A few weeks ago, when I was cleaning my 10-year-old son's room, I picked up a piece of notebook paper on which he had written, "What you send into the lives of others comes back into your own." I held that paper in my hands and felt immense gratitude that my son was learning the life lessons of Mary Kay.

Now I feel the same gratitude that I'm able to pass along not only to my children, but to women everywhere the life lessons of Mary Kay. This book grew from those lessons. In its preparation I reviewed the wisdom Mary Kay shared over the years in her speeches, books and loving conversations. Next I researched mountains of money-smart information from financial experts. And then as I looked back and forth at each, a funny thing happened. Right there in the middle of it all was a striking correlation between Mary Kay's living *right* principles and the financial experts' living *rich* advice. When the two merged—moral truths and money sense—the result was an unmistakable road map toward abundance . . . personal, financial and spiritual abundance.

So that's what you'll find here—a road map guided by Mary Kay's Laws of Living Rich that will not only broaden your mind and perhaps increase your net worth, but will also enrich your soul and uplift your spirit. Throughout the book you'll also find lessons and definitions in living rich shared by Mary Kay Independent Sales Directors and sidebars filled with bits of wisdom, surprising facts and key advice. Then, to reinforce your learning and encourage real action, the six most important things to do using the information you've just read will conclude each chapter.

You see, this book gets to the heart of the matter. It's not about appearances. It's about *being.* It's about *living.* It's about *you.* Enjoy!

—SHARON MORGAN TAHANEY

LIVING A RICH LIFE
Achieving Personal, Spiritual and Financial Abundance Following Mary Kay's Laws of Living Rich

Law # 1: Know Why

Law # 2: Know Yourself

Law # 3: Think Rich. Speak Rich. Act Rich

Law # 4: Balance It Out

Law # 5: Take the Long-term Look

Law # 6: Join the BIDIA (But I Did It Anyway) Club

Law # 7: Team Up

 # 8: Sow Good. Receive Good

Law # 9: Turn Stumbling Blocks into Stepping Stones

Law # 10: Begin Now

MARY KAY'S MISSION IS
TO ENRICH WOMEN'S LIVES.

We will do this in tangible ways,
by offering quality products to consumers,
financial opportunities to our independent sales force,
and fulfilling careers to our employees.

We will also reach out to the heart and spirit of women,
enabling personal growth and fulfillment
for the women whose lives we touch.

We will carry out our mission in a spirit of caring,
living the positive values on which our Company was built.

CONTENTS

Living a Rich Life

Living a Rich Life

CHAPTER ONE

Law #1: Know Why

How can people appear to have everything and yet be discontented? Perhaps they have stopped dreaming. I believe each of us needs a reason to get up in the morning. We need something to anticipate. . . something that truly excites us. —MARY KAY ASH

OVER 50 YEARS AGO, Antoine de Saint-Exupéry wrote *The Little Prince*, a story about a little prince who, through his interplanetary travels, learns the secret of what is really important in life. It's not easy to change someone's perspective on the world with a simple story, but this one can. While on his journey, the little prince meets a king for whom everyone is a subject. He meets a conceited man for whom everyone is an admirer. He meets a drunk who drinks to forget the shame of his drinking. He meets a businessman who has time only for "matters of consequence"— counting his possessions. He meets a geographer who knows the location of every sea, river, town, mountain and desert on his planet but has never seen one of them. Finally, the little prince lands on Earth and there meets a fox who shares with him the secret of life, an important truth—as it happens, the truth behind

Law #1. This truth is an inside-out kind of truth. To give you a hint, the author opens the story by showing a favorite drawing he made when he was 6. Here it is:

What do you see?

All the grown-ups he showed it to thought it was a hat. The 6-year-old artist knew that in reality the drawing was of a boa constrictor digesting an elephant.

The truth was there . . . you just couldn't see it. So the secret of life revealed by the fox? It's a big one. It's why we started with this particular law as the first one in this book. The secret was this: "One sees clearly only with the heart. Anything essential is invisible to the eye."[1]

What is essential in relationships, what is essential in growth, what is essential in happiness—all are invisible to the eye. And what is essential to a financial plan is just as invisible. It's called *purpose*. Without a purpose (the big reason *why*), the most efficient financial plan devised by the most proficient, highly credentialed financial planner on earth is doomed. With a purpose, however, your plan will have amazing power. You'll find the courage to get started and stick with it. You'll see the outcome as clearly as if you were already there. You'll feel the satisfaction of living your values and doing what you came here to do.

Your purpose is your driving vision. It is the "why" behind your plan. Knowing it is step one—Mary Kay's first law to living rich.

So how do you uncover your "why?" Let's begin by using the process of elimination. Is the purpose behind an efficient financial plan to have *more* and *bigger?* I can feel you shaking your head. I know you know the answer to that one. The treadmill of consumption is financially devastating. It's spiritually devastating. It's emotionally devastating. It's physically devastating. There's *always* more. There's *always* bigger. So is there ever success? Again your head is shaking. Of course not. Attaching material things to emotional needs is an empty process. If you feel worthless, a new suit and earrings won't change that reality. The outside will look good. The inside will still feel worthless. Knowing "why" is an inside-out kind of thinking. You can't see it. So obviously, it's not about stuff.

With every choice you make about money, ask yourself if it is consistent with what you've defined as values. If it isn't, move on. Don't waste your time or money on something that will give only a moment of pleasure. Remember, your goal is a lifetime of living rich.

What about money? Big piles of it. A bank vault full of it. Is the accumulation of money in its own right a sufficient purpose? Can money buy happiness? It can buy college educations. It can buy a secure neighborhood to raise your children. It can buy a good night's sleep the day the bills are due. Green pieces of paper then, in themselves, don't buy happiness. But as tools to achieve independence, security and peace of mind? You bet!

So let's talk about independence, security and peace of mind. These are examples of values . . . examples of *why*. To get a clear understanding of your values (your why), I'd like to ask you to do three things:

STEP ONE

Think of someone doing what you admire and identify her values represented in her actions.

I think we can all turn to Mary Kay Ash as someone whose actions clearly define her values—someone we admire, someone we would do well to emulate. Here are a few values she's made obvious in her life:

- Spiritual connection with God
- Love
- Learning
- Family
- Honesty
- Laughter
- Praise
- Challenges
- Independence
- Passion
- Enthusiasm
- Courage
- Self-expression
- Friendship
- Respect
- Making a difference
- Resourcefulness
- Selfless giving
- Belief
- Determination
- Persistence
- Balance
- Growth
- Teamwork
- Leadership
- Diligence
- Integrity
- Service
- Quality
- Praise
- Priorities

Do you see money anywhere on this list? No, because money is not a value. Can you see how living her values and sharing her values accomplished Mary Kay's purpose to change women's lives?

STEP TWO

Make your own list of values.

You will need a journal to collect your thoughts as you read this book. Keeping a journal is a nourishing thing to do anyway, so if you don't have one for jotting down moments of gratitude or special memories, make that investment now. The purchase will be well worth the cost.

In your journal, set aside a page for your values. First, think about how you currently spend your time and your money. People are drawn to activities and behaviors that satisfy feelings they value the highest. For instance, it's logical that the marathon runner values health, fitness and challenge. The socialite on every committee and on every guest list probably values acceptance, personal connection, making a difference. The workaholic possibly values power, status, action.

Now think about your "wants" and your current activities and translate those into the values they represent. This is more than a writing exercise in your journal. When you define your values, you'll begin changing your behavior to align with those values. Your spending habits will change. Your priorities will fall into place. You'll no longer jump into purchases counter to your values and wonder why they didn't really make you happy.

LESSON IN VALUES

My values are honesty, integrity, humility, the Golden Rule and a good work ethic. To live these values, I've had to be more disciplined in my spending. At first, I went a little crazy with spending the money I was making from my Mary Kay business. My mindset is now one of paying off debt before purchasing frivolous items. I teach my children the value of money and they do extra chores to earn stickers which turn into money (40 percent goes directly into savings).

—LEANNE SEXTON, Independent Senior Sales Director

Now spend the time—invaluable time—listing your most important values. Limit your list to ten or to your top five if having a set
number makes it easier to get started.
But do it. It feels great when you look
at those values on paper, and it will
feel even greater when you realize
you're fulfilling them. Think about it
. . . you've just given yourself a new
way to evaluate success. Instead of
feeling good only after you've
achieved a goal, you can feel good
every day you do *anything* that fulfills
your highest values. For example, instead of feeling good only after
you've lost those extra five pounds, you can feel good every time
you do anything that fulfills your value of health. Instead of cele-
brating only after you have $10,000 in an emergency fund, you
can celebrate every activity that fulfills your value of financial
security. Instead of feeling deprived when you save or sacrifice to
pay a debt, you can feel successful and enjoy the process when you
know with every payment you are achieving your values of independence, security and peace of mind. We're only human, right?
We typically continue doing only those things that make us feel
good. If we feel good, we stick with it. Sticking with it means ultimately mastering it and mastering it means getting to the finish
line—the big prize . . . the desired outcome. And the really great
thing? We've enjoyed the journey. We were fulfilled in the process,
so do you have those values down yet?

*Change your thinking
from being possession-
driven to being
commitment-driven.*

*As the life expectancy for women nears 90, you can expect
to live in retirement nearly 25 percent longer than men.*

—U.S. NATIONAL CENTER FOR HEALTH STATISTICS

STEP THREE

Own that list in your mind and heart.

Your standard for success is now in these values. Before every purchase, before you pull out that credit card, before you overcommit your time, measure that action against your list of values. Does it fulfill a value on your list? Or does it sabotage something there? Are you being proactive in fulfilling every value on that list? For instance, family may be high on your list. Do you have insurance and investments to support your family if you weren't around? Maybe independence was on your list. Do your current spending and saving habits match up with that value? If you're a little shaky about how you fulfill your values in money-smart ways, you'll feel more relaxed by the end of this book. We're talking "why" right now. We'll get into the "how" in Chapters 2 through 10.

Financial goals

Now it's time to translate values into financial goals. Where would you like to ultimately be? According to Tod Barnhart, in his book *A Kick in the Assets*,[2] life's five major financial goals are these:

1. "Burn your mortgage"
2. "Watch your children graduate"
3. "Become a millionaire"
4. "Do what you came here to do"
5. "Leave a legacy"

LESSON IN BACKING GOALS WITH PURPOSE

I can remember from my early years with Mary Kay people talking to me about goals, and that didn't impact me as it should have. My goals had to do with selling, selling so much product this week—that kind of goal. I usually reached those kinds of goals; however, when I put a reason behind the goal that was equally as powerful as the goal, then the goal never became work. Without a purpose behind a goal the process of reaching that goal becomes a burden. You'll focus on the work rather than the goal; consequently, the journey becomes unpleasant. I know for myself when my vision became larger than the goal, then the journey became a lot easier. For example, it was important to me to be able to be in a place in my life to take care of my parents. My father wasn't able to leave my mother the kind of money to provide her the quality of life she deserved as she aged. I had seen other people in this position. It was so bad, so frightening. I wanted to be financially independent to be able to change that for her. The place we wanted to be is what created the momentum—not just for my parents. The goal was to be financially independent so we could do the things for our children and people we loved. Those things became the goals of the journey; therefore, the journey became easy. People said, "You work so hard." To me, sure I worked hard, but it was not hard work because the overall vision was more powerful than the process of getting there. A lot of people make the mistake of establishing a "thing" goal that's not all encompassing. Whereas when your vision brings you to a place where many things are affected, then it becomes more of an all-encompassing goal. A goal has to have many different facets for it to truly be a rewarding goal. My mother today has dementia and if we were not in a position to take care of her, it would be horrible. We're able to afford quality nursing-home care. We've been able to keep up private insurance and specialty doctors. That was one of my strong purposes—it gave power to my goals, and now we are reaping the benefits of those purposes.

— CAROLYN WARD, Independent Executive National Sales Director

You've defined in your values and your "why" what you came here to do. Now let's look at these other four goals. How will it feel to achieve each one of these goals? Take the first one—burn your mortgage. If you're sitting at home right now, look around you. Now imagine how it will feel the day you no longer owe one solitary cent on your home. This piece of earth and the walls wrapped around you are all yours. That mortgage paper that governed your life for so long now means nothing. How does that feel? Can you match that feeling to a value on your list?

Now, let's imagine achieving financial goal number two—college graduation. There is your little angel walking across that stage in cap and gown and the biggest smile you've ever seen. There's the diploma. The handshake. You snap the picture, wipe the tear and wonder where the years went. How does it feel? You just gave your child a gift of independence and a real chance to realize personal goals. Congratulations! Now look back at your list of values. Is one of them glowing right now?

> *Sow a thought and you reap an act. Sow an act and you reap a habit. Sow a habit and you reap a character. Sow a character and you reap a destiny.*
>
> ANONYMOUS

Now, let's feel financial goal number three—become a millionaire. You've just turned 66. You open the mail and pull out your quarterly summary for your SEP account. There in the "Ending Value" box is the sum, $1,000,000. If the zeroes made you dizzy, let me clear it up for you—that's one *million* dollars. You take a deep breath, exhale and lean back in your chair. How does it feel? One million dollars is yours, which means so is security, respect and maybe a little adventure. Like that feeling? I do too, so the formula for accomplishing this million-dollar moment is in Chapter 5.

Now, financial goal number five—leaving a legacy. People mature dramatically on their deathbeds. Not a pleasant thought, but let's do what author Stephen Covey suggests, and begin with the end in mind. How do you want to be remembered? Your son or daughter is talking about you after you're gone. What do you want them to say? Again, if family was on your list of values, you not only want them to talk about the love you shared, but you also want them to feel the security and serenity you've left them. Leaving a legacy is not all about big-dollar inheritances. It's about being prepared for the inevitable in a way that leaves a legacy of peace after you're gone. Again, Chapter 5 will outline the basics in estate planning to address the financial side of achieving this goal.

Your financial goals

Now open your journal again and let's get personal. It's time to set a few goals for yourself. Here's the list. You decide what you want in each category. You may want to think in time frames. Look ahead five years. Look ahead ten years. Look ahead to retirement age.

- **Income.** What monthly income do you personally want to achieve within five years? Within ten years? The year before you retire?

- **Nest egg.** What dollar amount do you want to see in the "Value Box" on your investment accounts? Be a millionaire— why not! You are of royal lineage. You're a daughter of Mary Kay! Thinking small doesn't fit who you are.

- **Career achievement.** Who do you want to become in your Mary Kay business?

- **Possessions.** What do you want to own?

- **Experiences.** How about hiking the hills of Ireland? Or watching whales splash along the coast of Alaska? Or sitting in a seat of honor at your son's wedding? What do you want to experience in your lifetime?

LESSON IN SETTING GOALS

*M*y goals rarely became realities until I joined Mary Kay. When I learned to set a deadline and have a purpose and a plan of action, my goals surpassed my wildest dreams and became realities. How wonderful it's been to see my children follow my lead and become dream-builders excelling in all they do.

— JUNE WYLIE, Independent Executive Senior Sales Director

As Mary Kay has taught us, you can achieve anything if you believe you can and are willing to pay the price. If you *believe* you can. Think about that a minute. Belief is another one of those things you can't see but is essential to living a rich life. That conviction or trust or faith or whatever you wish to call belief is a bone-deep confidence that there is a greater hand at work here. It's a quiet understanding that turns a feverish search for happiness into an assured, relaxed state of being fulfilled, content . . . rich. You know . . . you simply know it will happen just as you've outlined it.

And guess what? As a bonus, it's been proven the state of believing actually improves our health! According to Harvard researcher Herb Benson, in his 1987 book *Beyond the Relaxation Response*,[3] when people believe in something—regardless of the nature of their belief—they are healthier. This force, the state of believing, seems to make the difference. So get the courage to actually believe you can accomplish all you wrote down as your goals. It's as good as an apple a day and even better for your prospects of living a rich life.

Six Most Important Things to Do to Know Why

1. Get a journal.

2. Think of someone you admire and jot down the values suggested by her actions.

3. Translate your current spending habits (time and money) into the values they suggest.

4. Make a list of your top five or top ten values.

5. Carry that list with you, post that list so you see it daily, own that list in your heart and mind.

6. List your financial goals in the areas of income, nest egg, career achievement, possessions and experiences.

Definitions of Living Rich

To have complete harmony and balance in life.
—*Rory McSweeney*

Being all you can be and to be paid what you're worth.
—*Sara Skaggs*

Having the vision, the belief and the faith to know you
can achieve whatever you really want or need.
—*Denise Montgomery*

A life of abundance with balance and flexibility.
—*Carol Fehr Dendle*

Freedom to enjoy it all.
—*Karen Colegary*

Truly enjoying each day.
—*Sherry L. Ray*

Surrounding myself with love and beauty.
—*Nancy Berman*

Being able to be a great wife, a great mother and enjoy what I do!
—*Kimbi Bartik*

Knowing that I can have access to all that I am willing to work for.
—*Gale Carter*

Living a Rich Life

CHAPTER TWO

Law #2: Know Yourself

You truly are wonderful and when God created you, He had a beautiful and special plan for your life. Believe in yourself. Have faith in yourself. Look for the best qualities in yourself. Believe that you are becoming the best that you can be. —MARY KAY ASH

TO BECOME THE BEST YOU CAN BE, you must know what *is* your best, you must know about money and you must know how the two of you coexist.

Of course, there's more to life than money. Certainly you live on a higher plain. But join me on the ground a minute because here are the facts: According to data from the U.S. Bureau of the Census, retired women live on just over half the income of retired men. Women live longer than men, have higher medical expenses, receive half the average pension benefits men do, are over three times more likely to be widowed than men and make up the staggering majority of single-parent families.

To compound this bleak picture, studies show that women know less about money management than men. In a 1992 Oppenheimer Management survey, 89 percent of women surveyed (vs. 69 percent of men) had no clue what the Dow Jones industrial average was, 77 percent (65 percent for men) didn't understand the relationship between interest rates and bonds, and 69 percent (53 percent for men) didn't know that stocks historically outperformed bonds, CDs and money markets.[1]

The word money *has a female origin. It was derived from the mythological Roman goddess Moneta, meaning riches, plenty and abundance.*

Put all these realities together and you have the recipe for what sociologists call "the feminization of poverty"—not what Mary Kay had in mind. Being poor makes it tough to be your best. So Law #2 suggests you not only know yourself but also your money. The better you get to know you and your money, the clearer it becomes that statistics don't dictate your destiny. Only *you* do that. Knowledge of who you are and what money is and isn't will give you the confidence to accept responsibility for your financial state and help shut down those "little girl" thoughts that you don't need or deserve much. It's a new millennium. Time for a new mindset. Time to make friends with money. Time to be your best.

To get to know you and your money, I'm going to ask you to put on two different thinking hats as you read this chapter. You're an expert at juggling hats, so this should be easy for you. Putting on a specific type of thinking hat to better understand a concept is the brainchild of a leading authority in the field of conceptual thinking, Dr. Edward de Bono.[2] In his book *Six Thinking Hats,* he suggests six hats when mulling over an idea. Today we will wear two of them, which are adapted from his ideas. First, we'll focus on the white hat, which directs our thinking toward the logical— the facts and figures that define your identity and that of money. Then we'll switch to the red hat and get the heart involved with an emotional view of who you are, what money is and the psychology behind your interaction.

See yourself in a white hat[3]

Slip on that white hat so you can take a purely logical, neutral look at where you stand and why you're there. To add to the depressing diatribe of stats outlined on the previous two pages, here are a few more appropriate for white-hat thinking:

- The median income of older persons in 1995 was $16,684 for males and $9,626 for females.
- Older women had a higher poverty rate (13.6 percent) than older men (6.8 percent) in 1996.
- The average age of widowhood is 56.
- Approximately 74 percent of women will be left on their own by separation, divorce, widowhood or the choice of single life.
- Three out of five poor adults are women.
- Three out of four working women earn less than $25,000 per year.
- Nine out of ten working women earn less than $40,000 a year.
- Women's earnings average 74 cents for every $1 earned by men—a lifetime loss of over $250,000.

So far, the look from under this white hat is none too flattering. Why have men and women had such different experiences with money? Is there really such a difference between men and women to contribute to this kind of spread?

Neurophysiologists and cognitive psychologists argue that gender differences are due to the simple fact that men and women are wired to think and feel differently. (It took a doctorate degree to tell us that?) But let's take a closer, white-hatted look. These bio-differences could clear up a few things. According to *Science* magazine in 1995, University of Chicago researchers who analyzed 32 years of standardized testing results found boys outnumbered girls by three to one in the top 10 percent in mathematics. However, the girls smoked the boys on the verbal side of the tests with significantly superior writing skills and twice as many girls in the top of reading comprehension. What does this say to us about money? Here's a woman's take: We *have* to understand the numbers. We *must* deal with budgets and net-worth calculations. But our real power in money management is focusing on the human connection with those numbers. What does having a spending plan mean in emotional benefits? Here we go again back into the importance of values and purpose to guide our money decisions. This isn't soft-headed, emotional foo-foo. This is power . . . real understanding of who we are and how to make the most of our strengths.

> *In 1972, women earned 57.9 percent of men's earnings. In 1997, women turned that percentage into 74.2 percent.*
>
> U.S. BUREAU OF THE CENSUS

Before we move on, just a word of caution. Biodifferences suggest a money style—not a money outcome. Recognizing that men and women think and feel differently is not an excuse to hand over money decisions to the resident male. It's an explanation why some aspects of money management may feel foreign. It's an encouragement to continue on anyway. It's a signpost pointing toward your strengths.

See yourself in a red hat[4]

Remove your white hat and slip on the bright red one. Now your view will be different. Red-hat thinking allows emotion into the picture. We can see that money is an energy, that we have a money personality, and the way we handle money has to do with thinking patterns common to a lot of people. By slipping on a red hat, we can take a better look at money for what it is and at how we relate to it.

First, before we look more closely at your money personality, let's examine money itself. Joseph Campbell, noted mythologist and thinker, defined money as "congealed energy." That seems to be the consensus of many noted authors of personal finance books. Money is a force that is repelled by certain behaviors and attracted by others. An attitude of easy-come, easy-go sends money flying out of your possession. A respect for the value of money, on the other hand, attracts more money to you. Warren Buffett, one of the top five wealthiest people in this country, is known for stooping down and picking up a penny—a sign of obvious respect. The key to accumulating wealth is not the penny, it is the respect.

LESSON IN RESPECT

I used to hoard money in a little box when I was young. I would count it every day, fearing it would be stolen or lost or taken away. These were my little "talents," and when I was young, I hid them. As I grew, I became more irresponsible with my money, amassing large credit-card debt—almost $100,000! Separated, unhappy and poor, I looked to Mary Kay for some answers. Mary Kay pointed me toward God. First, He taught me how to be responsible with the "talents" He gave me. Rebuilding my confidence, reducing my debt, teaching me how to be a good steward of His money—these are the benefits of faith and a career with Mary Kay. Today, I have less respect for money as a "thing" to acquire and more respect for it as a tool. The debt is down to $27,000.

—ANNE JOHNS, Independent Senior Sales Director

This kind of intangible that gives value to money was also recognized by the Federal Reserve Bank in Chicago in an October 1982 article in *Modern Money Mechanics*. See if you can find it: "In the United States, neither paper currency nor deposits have value as commodities. Intrinsically, a dollar bill is just a piece of paper. Deposits are merely book entries. What then makes these instruments—checks, paper money, and coins—acceptable at face value in payment of all debts and for other monetary uses? Mainly, it is the *confidence* people have that they will be able to exchange such money for other financial assets and real goods and services whenever they choose to do so. . . ."

I know that was dry reading. I apologize. The point made, however, is important. What gives money its value in the big scheme of economic policy? The answer is in one word: *confidence.* Most people think of money as a tangible object that can be moved around in different accounts and in color-coordinated handbags. The reality, however, is that most money isn't available as cash.

Life expectancy at age 65 increased by 2.4 years between 1900 and 1960, but has increased by 3.4 years since 1960.

U.S. BUREAU OF
THE CENSUS

Think about this—there are approximately $266,902,367,798 U.S. dollars in existence in bills. That means less than $1,000 is available for each of the 271 million U.S. citizens. You see, most of the money doesn't physically exist. It's a book entry. It is real as currency because of our *confidence* that it's real—the same confidence that will create money in your own life.

How? Confidence can *save* you money and can *make* you money. For example, use it to negotiate. Ask for a lower price when you're purchasing something. In other words, ask for what you want. You may hear "no," but you are more likely to get what you want if you aren't afraid to ask for it. Confidence is simply a belief in your abilities. Accumulating financial wealth starts with this belief—the confidence to know you deserve more and are perfectly capable of achieving it.

> **LESSON IN BREAKING FALSE BARRIERS**
>
> When I was growing up, choice and abundance were never a reality in our family. Both my parents grew up during the Depression when limited thinking and making the best of nothing were evident. Learning the power of choice and increasing my deserve level has been a life-long challenge. Breaking those false barriers has been a constant challenge for me. My greatest desire is to break the chain of self-limiting thought patterns for my children and grandchildren.
>
> —**PAM PEARSON**, Independent Senior Sales Director

So let's dig a little deeper in examining your emotional take on money. A growing science called behavioral finance identifies the psychological causes behind many of our money decisions. The idea is if you can understand the patterns of thought and behavior that lead to destructive choices, you'll be able to get rid of them and make more money while keeping more of what you have. One of the most common emotional traps that leads to poor money decisions is the tendency to value some dollars less than others. Behavioral economists call this "mental accounting."

For example, compare gift income to earned income. Your mother-in-law sends $50 in your birthday card. Found money, right? Do you feel the same way about that $50 as the $50 you earned from a skin-care class? Which one are you more likely to go out and blow on the first thing that catches your eye at the mall?

Harmless enough, you say. And you're right. The harm comes when this same kind of mental accounting becomes a consistent part of your spending patterns. Take your tax return, for instance. When you get that refund, do you spend it more freely than if you had taken that same amount of your check each month and deposited it into a savings account? At the end of the year, would you be as likely to spend your savings account?

Mental accounting also means you value money differently depending on how you're *spending* it—with cash, with check or with credit card. Checks are not as tangible as cash. Proof positive is the fact that scads of them are out there bouncing around and thousands more are being written at this very moment without a thought to a bank balance. And credit! The ultimate in cheapened money! It's so easy. There's no sense of loss at the time of purchase, so you can end up spending money you may not have ordinarily spent. Money is cheapened to the point that the average U.S. consumer with revolving credit has more than $7,000 in credit-card debt.

Gary Belsky and Thomas Gilovich, in their 1999 book, *Why Smart People Make Big Money Mistakes*,[5] provide a perfect example of how mental accounting can wreck a savings plan when you treat dollars differently depending on the size of the transaction. What would you do in their example?

> Imagine that you go to a store to buy a lamp, which sells for $100. At the store you discover that the same lamp is on sale for $75 at a branch of the store five blocks away. Do you go to the other branch to get the lower price?
>
> Now imagine that you go to the same store to buy a dining room set, which sells for $1,775. At the store you discover that you can buy the same table and chairs for $1,750 at a branch of the store five blocks away. Do you go to the other branch to get the lower price?

Studies say more people will go the five blocks to save the $25 on the lamp than would go the same five blocks to save $25 on the dining room set. It's the same $25, but it's valued differently because of the size of the transaction. The same holds true with payments you receive when the dollar-size is reversed. For example, suppose you receive a fairly small bonus in the amount of $75. Chances are excellent you'll treat that $75 casually and spend it freely, whereas if that bonus had been $750, it would have become serious money to you and probably would have been deposited into your account and handled with more care.

Understanding this tendency toward "mental accounting" may clear up your confusion as to why you can't seem to save money. Maybe you have been doing a little mental accounting, treating money in the slush fund casually or buying extra things at the grocery store without thinking—a dollar here, a dollar there. According to Belsky and Gilovich,[6] here are the warning signs that show you may be "prone to mental accounting":

- You don't think you're a reckless spender, but you have trouble saving.
- You have savings in the bank *and* revolving balances on credit cards.
- You're more likely to splurge with a tax refund than with savings.
- You seem to spend more when you use credit cards than when you pay with cash.
- Most of your retirement funds are in fixed-income or other conservative investments.

To counteract these psychological money traps, some financial experts suggest you:

- Try a month without plastic and use only cash to pay for all your purchases. Do you spend the same amount?
- After that month, ask yourself before any credit-card purchase, "How much would I pay for this item if I were paying cash out of my purse?"
- Another tip is to put any earnings or bonuses you receive into your bank account and commit to leaving them there for at least 48 hours before you touch them.

- Some say "found" money should stay in your account for at least three to six months. By depositing it into your account, it becomes *yours*. You claim it and are much less likely to spend it frivolously.

- Another counterattack to mental accounting is to imagine all income as *earned* income. Ask yourself how long it would take you to earn that amount of money. Think in terms of trading your time for that purchase. Still worth it?

- Here's a great tip: put mental accounting to work in your favor. Use an automatic deduction plan so that $50 you would have easily spent carelessly will go into an investment and turn into serious money.

LESSON IN BEING DILIGENT AND SYSTEMATIC

While building my Mary Kay business, I've moved five times, been through three major surgeries, have picked myself up from divorce. Because of the Mary Kay philosophy, love and education, I've raised two wonderful, independent, goal-oriented children. I've also learned to be systematic in my approach to this business. We as women need to be smart with taxes and money management. My goal is to empower women to be great business leaders and help others achieve their goals. We need to be savvy with what we're doing. We all need to know exactly what we can and can't do when it comes to filing taxes, and if we don't know, we're leaving money on the table. I have a business plan, I work with Invesco* and I take 15 percent of my commission check each month for savings. This covers my travel and my tax payments. I make it simple by automatically deducting this set amount from my commission check. I don't see the money so I don't spend it. My advice to others is to have people do your taxes who are familiar with home-based businesses. Know what you can and can not deduct and document your business correctly. Take advantage of automatic deductions and work diligently.

— CONNIE KITTSON, Independent Senior Sales Director

---

* Mary Kay Inc. does not endorse Invesco or in any way warrant, represent or guarantee the safety or the rate of return of any investment with Invesco.

Wearing a red hat to make decisions

According to Henry S. Brock, in his book *Your Complete Guide to Money Happiness,*[7] the biggest roadblock to living rich as we've defined it in this book is ego. Pure and simple ego. Basing decisions on satisfying the ego means focusing on things combined with instant gratification. An ego-based decision is prefaced by the thought, "What would others think?" An ego-driven person worries about the short term and is driven by competition and pride.

A person driven by the desire to live rich is a person who asks, "What can I do for others?" She thinks long-term and win-win. To clarify the different thought processes at work, here is Henry Brock's outline of the decision-making criteria for each kind of person.

HAPPINESS CRITERIA FOR LIVING RICH

Focus on relationships

Experiences that yield fulfillment

Joy

Peace

Happiness

"What can I do for others?"

Thinks long-term

Builds up others

Helps others and cooperates

Serves

Abundance mentality

Thinks win-win

Centered on others

Sacrifices something of the moment for something
wanted later

Balances spending with saving

Enjoys freedom

Not addicted to spending and debt

Sees money as stewardship

Spends time and money on family memories, adequate success and high balance

EGO CRITERIA FOR LIVING IN-THE-MOMENT

Focus on things

Experiences that yield pleasure

Fun

Entertainment

Instant gratification

"What will others think?"

Worries about the short-term

Puts others down

Competition and pride

Egocentric

Scarcity mentality

Thinks win-lose

Inward-centered

Sacrifices what he/she wants most for what he/she wants now

Spends and consumes

In bondage

Slave to debt

Money is trivial, "easy-come, easy-go"

Strives for excessive achievement

Get to know your money personality

Henry S. Brock also says there are basically only two types of people when it comes to money:

Type 1: the type who spends first and saves later

Type 2: the type who saves first and spends later

He reports that 19 out of 20 people are Type 1 and only one out of 20 is Type 2. Which are you?

To further define your money style, have some fun and jot down your answers in the little quiz that follows. You may want to use another sheet of paper so your husband can take the test later. The results can make you more comfortable with your money style and may help you become more flexible and willing to move to a more neutral position.

1. **If I received a $4,500 tax refund, my first impulse would be to**

   A. put it in a passbook savings account.

   B. send it to my favorite charity.

   C. invest it in a stock that looks promising.

   D. think about all the options that must be available for that money and decide to decide later.

   E. splurge on a spending spree for me and my family.

2. **When it comes to a spending plan or budget, I**

   A. actually take pride in sticking to the plan.

   B. don't have enough variable expenses to really worry about having one.

   C. keep a copy on my computer and redo it often.

   D. never bothered with one.

   E. find a budget impossible to follow.

3. **Regarding expenditures, I**

   A. don't enjoy spending money—I'd much rather see my money grow in a savings account.

   B. don't keep up with them. Tracking every penny is majoring in the minors of life as far as I'm concerned.

   C. love spending money as long as I am also saving it.

   D. keep my fingers crossed that I don't get blindsided by an unexpected expense.

   E. have a blast spending money.

4. **On the subject of credit cards, I**

   A. never use them. I believe in sticking to cash.

   B. don't care for credit cards and use them only when I have to.

   C. use credit cards for their convenience. I pay the balance off each month and use the statements to categorize my spending habits and prepare for my income-tax reports.

   D. can't seem to keep up with that monthly payment deadline. Before I know it, the next month's statement has come and I haven't paid the last one.

   E. absolutely adore credit cards! I have one in every color!

5. **As far as connecting emotions and money, I**

   A. never think of spending money as a way to make me happy or get over a sad event.

   B. have found that spending money just makes me feel worse.

   C. feel happier when I'm seeing my money grow rather than when I'm spending it.

   D. don't see how the two connect whatsoever.

   E. seem to feel better when I'm spending money.

AND THE RESULTS

Mostly A answers: You have a Silas Marner mentality—you like to hang tight to your money. You take pride in your self-discipline.

B answers: You have a righteous attitude about money. You roll your eyes at the whole subject of budgets and money matters. Your cavalier attitude helps you cover up the fear and uneasiness money inspires in you.

C answers: You have a pretty healthy attitude about money. You like seeing it grow, are not afraid to spend it or invest it. You take the offensive when it comes to credit cards and use them responsibly.

D answers: You ignore the whole subject of money management. You're above the details of balancing checkbooks and saving receipts. The whole thing bores you silly.

E answers: Tilt! You're a spender! Shopping is an art form—and you're the maestro. The sales clerks in the local mall know you by name. A number of credit-card companies are considering making you an honorary board member.

According to a study by the Department of Labor, a staggering 99 percent of women in America will work for pay sometime during their lives.

LESSON IN FINDING MYSELF

I went through a divorce which was devastating at the time but ultimately taught me valuable lessons about who I am. First, I learned that a woman's confidence can't come from someone else. It must come from within. In other words, a woman has to be accountable for herself spiritually, emotionally and financially. Quickly after my divorce I went through my $20,000 in savings in a few months. I realized during this time that I really wasn't clear about who I was. I thought I was this independent businesswoman. I had been married to a professional man; we were living well and enjoying life. Then when I got divorced, I felt a huge emotional void. I had to do some soul-searching about who I was, what I believed, and how I could be confident about who I was. Intellectually I understood I was an independent businesswoman, but I didn't understand it experientially. Then when I went through this, things started to make sense. The mistake many women make in developing relationships is they tend to look for a person to fulfill the part of themselves that is missing. Two halves come together in a relationship instead of two wholes. I learned that you need to be two wholes to have a good relationship. The next lesson I learned was when something like this happens, you need to allow yourself to feel the pain, to observe it and become spiritually centered in order to have strength to go beyond it. I started the healing process by pulling myself together spiritually. I got saved and got my relationship with God right. I realized that my confidence comes from Him, not from another individual. From there I began to understand my responsibilities financially—how to save money, how to get my retirement plan in place, how to manage my own credit cards and move up in my career. The third lesson I learned about myself during this time was that to truly heal and be independent, you need to be open about your feelings. You need to share the truth about your situation with others. The most important lesson I learned about myself was that rather than choosing to be a victim, I choose to be victorious. I hope you do too!

— CONNIE PHILLIPS, Independent National Sales Director

One more look at yourself and your money

Now that you've looked from under the brim of your white hat at the statistics and trends describing women and switched to your red hat to see yourself in light of thinking patterns and personality styles, it's time for one more self-defining exercise. To see clearly where you are now and where you want to go from here, it's important you take a reflective look back. We are all shaped from things and people and significant moments in our past. What are those moments for you?

I took a few minutes to glance backward and conduct this self-defining exercise for myself. Here is my look back:

Where I'm From

I'm from scrubbed kitchen floors and vegetable gardens

From Tupperware bowls and cancer crusades

I'm from gravel and trees and Arkansas farmland

From Church of God pews and Christmas-time plays

I'm from Mother's strong eyes and Daddy's soft shoulder

From basketball games and gospel quartets

I'm from butterbean rows and Emerson's Woodnotes

Sisterly love and boy-next-door dates

I'm from student loans, old cars, odd jobs and lit. books

Government grants and professor reviews

I'm from classrooms and boardrooms; chalkboards and keyboards

Black type and white space and manuscript proofs

I'm from my sons' laughter and constant boy chatter,

Mary Kay's Go-Give and love's butterfly wings

I'm from all these moments. Shaped by this history.

Bit by bit formed from these tiniest of things.

We're forged from our past but share in our future

Destined to realize whatever we choose

Let's go there together; let's laugh there together

And be soulfully rich . . . this moment too.

—SHARON MORGAN TAHANEY

Now open your journal and create your own "Where I'm From" poem. Don't worry about rhyming the words or keeping the lines in rhythm. Just capture the bits and pieces of your past that have made you who you are. Feel free to use my last verse as your last verse too and we will live rich together in a beautiful, creative moment.

So slow down, get a cup of coffee, sit back and relive your life. Then enjoy this view of you. It's sure to be a satisfying one and the perfect grounding experience before moving on to Chapter 3.

Statistics rate finances to be the number-three priority in life.
This is after love (number one) and work (number two).

—GERI FERNET, "PRIORITIZING YOUR FINANCES."
WWW.WOMENTODAYMAGAZINE.COM.,
AUGUST 10, 1999.

Six Most Important Things to Do to Know Yourself and Your Money

1. Respect yourself. Respect your money. Pick up spare coins and collect them in a jar. When the jar is full, apply the total to an investment fund.

2. Deal with money with complete and total *confidence*. Know you will achieve every one of your financial goals.

3. Be aware of "mental accounting" traps. When you spot them in your thinking, stop and ask yourself if you would pay the same amount in cash. Think of the amount you're spending as "earned income."

4. Look back over the list of "Happiness Criteria for Living Rich." Incorporate each characteristic into your everyday life.

5. If you're not there yet, move into Type 2 as your preferred money style—save first, spend later. Take the money personality test. Apply your new understanding of your money style to the material you read in the rest of this book.

6. Create your "Where I'm From" poem. Read it to someone special and smile.

Definitions of Living Rich

To have a heart so full of the love from sisters in this Company
that we *never* feel alone.
—*Boni Tucker*

Being surrounded by caring people, having an abundant lifestyle
and sharing it with others.
—*Annie Chapman*

Having total control over my time— the time I want for my church,
the time I want for my family and the time I want for my young
nieces whose mother recently died.
—*Denise Kucharski*

Quality time with family.
—*Ruth Magrini*

Being able to take care of my parents and family.
—*Donna Hammett*

Being able to enjoy all the areas of my life without sacrificing
anything.
—*O'nelly Encarnacion*

Surrounding myself with love and beauty.
—*Nancy Berman*

Being surrounded by goal-setting, exciting, positive, faith-filled
women and leaving my mark.
—*Joyce Hubert*

Peace within myself and the ability to know personal relationships
are more valuable than money.
—*Jane Sloper-Berg*

Living a Rich Life

CHAPTER THREE

Law #3: Think Rich. Speak Rich. Act Rich

Realize that the dominating thoughts of your mind eventually reproduce themselves in outward bodily action and gradually transform themselves into physical reality. Get rid of words like "I can't . . . but . . . what if," and exchange them for "I can. I will. I must." Act successful, and you will draw success to you. We are surrounded by abundance and we can draw it to us by expecting it.

—MARY KAY ASH

WHAT YOU *THINK* ABOUT, YOU *BRING* ABOUT. Simple enough. Even catchy. But the trick is this: Take these words off the page and live them. Actually think about who you want to become tomorrow, who you want to become ten years from now, who you want to become when you're 66. Think about what you want to own, what you want to give, what you want to experience. Think about how you want to live when you have grandchildren to visit. *Think* about it. *Talk* about it. *Act* each day in a way that moves you toward that image. Then watch out! The reality of your thoughts will materialize in your mirror. It's a law. It will happen.

Think rich

So let's start with the thinking part. The mind is a glorious gift. It can store all kinds of hard data to be retrieved whenever you need it—real things like to-do lists and career path status and product ingredients. And, on top of all those facts and figures, the mind can do what the biggest, baddest, giggabyting computer *can't* do. It can imagine. It can dream. A subplot unfolds in your brain that gives real power and meaning to the events and characters running around on the conscious level. The first imperative of Law #3, therefore, is a two-part process. It involves: 1) thinking rich on the conscious level; and 2) thinking rich on the subconscious level.

The term blue chip *was created from a 19th-century poker game. The blue chip was considered to be the one with the highest value.*

Let's take the conscious level first. This is where we jump onto a learning curve so we can know what rich people know. You may remember that in *The Great Gatsby*, F. Scott Fitzgerald proclaims that the rich are different from you and me. But the truth is, they're not really different; they just know more about money. This is your chance to change that fact. Here is a compilation of what you absolutely need to know about money in order to live rich in understanding. We're only dealing with money understanding here. You're on your own understanding why your kids collect Pokémon™ cards and your husband refuses to let go of the remote control. This section will, however, help you understand the financial section of your newspaper. Investment commercials on TV will begin to make sense, and *The Wall Street Journal* can be as natural for you to pick up as a *Chicken Soup* book.

The investing evolution

So here goes. Let's begin with a little history lesson. By looking back at our grandparents and parents and the events that shaped their retirement planning, we will see how the past created the present and how we can use that knowledge to prepare for the future.

We'll go back as far as the **GI Generation (born 1902–24)** and take a look at how it handled retirement planning. In 1920, the federal government instituted an employee pension system and in 1935 Social Security was formed. The youngest of this GI Generation was 14 years old at the time. The oldest was 34. It made sense to them, then, that their retirement needs would be covered under the safety net of these two retirement initiatives. The government and their employers would provide.

Then came the **Silent Generation (born 1925–42).** This generation believed, as its parents did, that Social Security and pension plans were the answer to retirement. In their formative years they witnessed the first monthly Social Security check (1940) issued to May Fuller of Ludlow, Vermont. She had paid $24.75 in Social Security tax and received a lifetime benefit of $22,889. What a godsend this Social Security! They also saw Congress vote to increase Social Security benefits while a full 41 percent of them were assured of a set amount of cash for life thanks to their employers' pension plans. However, there was another influence that shifted their thinking toward at least partial participation in the savings side of their retirement plan—World

Here's a statistic that will build your patience for a buy-and-hold strategy: The Dow Jones Industrial Average experienced swings of greater than 100 points 52 times in 1997.

War II. World War II left the Silent Generation not quite so silent. Following the war, nearly 20 million Americans (almost 20 percent of the population) became individual investors—primarily in government bonds. The investing evolution officially began.

Next entered the **Baby Boomer Generation (born 1943–60).** The shaping of retirement planning for this generation had conflicting influences. In 1965, the Medicare Bill providing health insurance for those 65 and over went into effect. In 1972, Congress raised Social Security benefits by 20 percent and voted in automatic cost-of-living adjustments. Then in 1978, an opposite event occurred that opened the door for self-responsibility. Section 401(k) of the Revenue Act of 1978 entered the scene. Now, for the first time, employees could decide if and how much to contribute to retirement savings (sometimes with a partial match from their employers). Regular folks began to explore investment options and think about saving for retirement on their own. And while these Baby Boomers were investigating mutual funds and getting concerned about government help in their golden years, a new bill was passed in 1983 that made Social Security benefits taxable and raised the eligibility age all the way up to age 67 for those born in 1960 or later. At the same time, computations flooded the Social Security Administration showing how this boom of retirees would strain the system. Social Security didn't seem to have as much security anymore. Then to

Legendary investor Warren Buffett once wrote to the shareholders of his holding company, Berkshire Hathaway Inc., that "you would have been better off last year if I had regularly snuck off to the movies during the market hours." Even the pros goof when trying to time the market.

top off the erosion of confidence in the system, in 1986, mandatory retirement was abolished. It was almost as if the government were pleading, "Keep working! Please take care of yourself!" Understandably, retirement inched up on the Baby Boomer list of things to stress out about. Consequently, individual investing evolved once again.

Then the Internet hit. What an incredible difference the Net made in individual responsibility! To begin a new century, there were over 11,000 investing Web sites. According to Gomez Advisors, an e-commerce research firm, by the year 2001, investors will have opened 18 million Internet brokerage accounts, up from the 7.1 million they opened in 1998. A new financial order had emerged. Individuals could no longer rely on the government or their employers. The realization came clear—the buck stops here. Or in the case of retirement planning, the buck *starts* here . . . with me . . . with you . . . with anyone who plans to avoid eating cat food as a retirement staple.

Now, the knowledge

FIRST, CLEARING UP THE FINANCIAL NEWS

This section covering economic know-how won't make you an expert. It will, however, clear the fog-surrounding terms you hear every day in the news—the ones you dismissed as having absolutely no relevance in your life. That was poverty thinking. It's time to flip the switch and learn. So take your time here and really think as you read these explanations taken from literature by the U.S. Securities and Exchange Commission and the Barron's book, *Keys to Understanding the Financial News,*[1] which was the source for all the quoted material in this section. If you truly want to think rich, you have to be able to interpret financial news with common sense and confidence. Then when you hear these terms on the news or in conversation, instead of nodding off or heading out, you will understand.

Gross Domestic Product

This was called the Gross National Product (GNP) until 1992 when the U.S. changed from GNP accounting to GDP (Gross Domestic Product). Gross Domestic Product (GDP) "represents the total market value of the final output of a nation's goods and services produced within the boundaries of [our country. Simply, it is the] principal measure of [our] output. . . . The GDP is [said to be] the broadest single measure of U.S. economic activity and is usually considered to be the best available indicator of the economy's health." GDP reports are presented on an annual basis in percentage changes.

Leading economic indicators

The U.S. Department of Commerce publishes three indicators of business activity around the first of each month:

1. the index of "Lagging Economic Indicators" showing what has happened;

2. the index of "Coincident Economic Indicators" showing what is happening currently; and

3. the index of "Leading Economic Indicators," statistics that point toward future economic movement. This is the index that gets most of the media attention since most investors are interested in the future picture rather than a current or past one. The indicators in this index are the following:

    1. average weekly hours paid to production workers in manufacturing
    2. average weekly claims for unemployment insurance
    3. new orders for consumer goods and materials
    4. index of 500 common stock prices
    5. contracts and orders for new plant equipment
    6. index of building permits for new private housing units
    7. vendor performance—slower deliveries index
    8. change in index of sensitive materials

9. money supply [currency in circulation plus checking accounts, money market, mutual funds, short-term deposits and CDs

10. change in manufacturers' unfilled orders (in 1982 dollars)

11. index of consumer expectations

"The Index of Leading Economic Indicators can be thought of as a useful but not totally reliable predicting tool," according to *Keys to Understanding the Financial News.* "[Although not always true,] the rule of thumb is that three successive monthly declines, or increases, in the index indicate the economy will soon turn in the same direction . . . monthly moves in the index are not as important as cumulative long-run trends."

According to Ibbotson Associates (a company specializing in financial statistics), common stocks have provided a compound annual return of 16.3 percent between 1976 and 1998.

WWW.IBBOTSON.COM

Inflation

Inflation is defined as a rise in the general level of prices. Since, realistically, price changes for all goods we produce can't be computed, statisticians for the federal government have selected a representative basket of goods and compute the price changes of the market basket each month. What does inflation mean to you? Inflation can cause a lender to lose money. (You are the lender if you buy a corporate bond—you are essentially lending the corporation the amount of money of your bond.) "If $10,000 is borrowed for one year and the inflation rate for that year is 5 percent, the dollars of principal repaid at the end of the year have depreciated by 5 percent. . . . The borrower benefits by repaying less real dollars while the lender receives dollars whose purchasing power has declined. Inflation can also have a negative effect on savings. As prices rise, the value of savings will decline if the rate of inflation exceeds the rate of interest," the book explains. As far as how inflation affects your investments, here is a general rule of thumb: During times of decelerating or stable inflation, financial assets such as stocks and bonds are the superstars. During times of accelerating inflation, real assets such as real estate and precious metals are the winners.

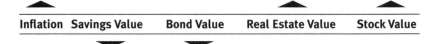

| Inflation | Savings Value | Bond Value | Real Estate Value | Stock Value |

Consumer Price Index (CPI)

This index is one of the tools used to measure inflation rates and is the most widely cited index in the news. "It attempts to measure changes in prices of goods and services purchased by urban consumers. The Bureau of Labor Statistics computes the index monthly based on data collected in 85 cities on price changes of approximately 400 goods and services in seven categories: food, clothing, housing, transportation, medical care, entertainment, and other. The CPI is considered the most reliable measure of changes in the cost of living. . . ."

Federal Reserve System

OK, stay with me here. This gets complex, but since this organization is in the news and has such powerful impact on interest rates, you should know its meaning. "The Federal Reserve System . . . includes the Board of Governors of the Federal Reserve System, the Federal Open Market Committee, and the 12 regional Federal Reserve Banks. The Federal Reserve (Fed) is the central bank [whose most important responsibility is the] control of the money supply. . . . At the top of the Federal

Reserve's organization structure is the Board of Governors. . . . The seven members of the Board are appointed by the U.S. President and confirmed by the Senate. All appointments are for 14-year terms. . . . The President also designates the chairman and vice-chairman who serve for four-year terms. . . . The chairman of the Board occupies a powerful position often cited as being second only to the President."

Money supply

"The supply of money is of critical importance to economic activity. . . . The control of the money supply is the main responsibility of the Fed. An increase in the money supply relative to demand for it causes interest rates to fall, stimulating investment spending, output, and employment. . . . When more money exists than is needed to carry out transactions, inflation will also result." That's when the Federal Reserve Board steps in to raise interest rates to slow down the spending and curtail inflation.

Bulls believe stock prices are going to rise. Bears believe stock prices are going to fall. You can ignore both by using dollar-cost averaging.

Interest rates

This is "the price a borrower pays for the use of a lender's money." Two critical interest rates that eventually affect the interest rate you pay to borrow money are 1) Federal Funds Rate (set by the Federal Reserve, this is "the rate banks have to pay to borrow reserves from other banks"), and 2) Prime Rate, "the rate charged by commercial banks to their most creditworthy customers." (When the Fed raises the interest rate the banks are charged to borrow money, guess what happens to the rate the bank charges you?) Higher interest rates slow the economy to fend off a high rise in inflation. Now do you see how the Fed impacts your life?

Fiscal policy vs. monetary policy

Fiscal policy is set by the federal government and is implemented through taxation and government spending. Monetary policy is set by the Federal Reserve Board and is expressed by the rise and fall of interest rates.

Unemployment

Unemployment is measured by computing the average weekly claims for unemployment insurance. Economists rely heavily on this indicator to signal future business activity.

The market

According to the *American Fund Investor,* "when people refer to 'the market,' they usually mean the U.S. stock market." The stock market in its simplest form represents ownership of corporate America.

Bull vs. bear

Bulls believe stock or the stock market is going up in price. Bears believe it is going down. One theory to the origin of these terms is in the way the actual bull and bear attack. The bear rakes down with his large claws, whereas the bull tosses up his large sharp horns.

Securities and Exchange Commission (SEC)

The Securities and Exchange Commission is like the cop on the beat on Wall Street. This U.S. agency administers the federal laws that protect investors. The SEC was created after the Great Depression of the 1930s to restore confidence in the securities market.

Stocks

Stock represents ownership of a piece of a company and is traded in units known as shares. Stock shares are bought and sold on the stock market. Share prices will rise on a certain stock if many people want to buy that particular stock. If more people want to sell the stock, the share price will fall.

Common stock

Common stock represents part ownership in the company and may or may not provide a dividend.

Preferred stock

Preferred stock provides a fixed dividend and does not participate in the growth of a company. In this regard, it is more like a bond. It is also different from common stock due to certain preferential rights. "Preferred stockholders have priority in receiving dividend income and claims on company assets in case of dissolution." Just as a note, if a company does get into financial difficulty, the interest due to bondholders takes precedence over the dividend claims of preferred stockholders.

Stock exchanges

A stock exchange is the physical location where stocks are traded. "Common stocks are traded primarily on nine stock exchanges in the United States. The largest stock exchange is the New York Stock Exchange (NYSE). . . . A smaller version of the NYSE is the American Stock Exchange (Amex) also located in Manhattan's financial district. These two are considered national exchanges. Common stock is also traded on seven major regional exchanges. . . . The largest of the regional exchanges is the Midwest Stock Exchange located in Chicago."

OTC market

"The term *over-the-counter* (OTC) originated when securities were traded over the counters in stores of various dealers from their inventory of securities." Now the term has nothing to do with a centralized trading floor where all orders are processed like the NYSE and the Amex. OTC trading is conducted through a computer-telephone network of dealers across the country.

NASDAQ

"In 1917 The National Association of Securities Dealers (NASD)—the organization of security dealers that regulates the OTC market—started providing stock price quotations through its system called the National Association of Securities Dealers Automatic Quotations (NASDAQ) system."

Dow Jones Industrial Average (DJIA)

"The DJIA is the most widely followed stock market average. The Index was first calculated by Charles Dow in 1884 by adding together the prices of 11 important stocks and dividing the total by 11. The average was broadened in 1928 to include 30 stocks and the composition [of this 30-company barometer] has been updated over the years." Companies included in the Dow index are some of the oldest publicly traded companies in America and are considered "blue chips" because of their strength and stability. Examples include the Walt Disney Company, AT&T, McDonald's Corporation, Eastman Kodak and the Coca-Cola Company.

Standard & Poor's 500 Stock Index

"The S&P 500 is, next to the DJIA, the most widely followed barometer of stock market movements." Because it is a larger sample size (500 stocks within the leading industries), the S&P 500 "is more representative of the movement of the stock market as a whole."

Growth stocks

Growth stocks are stocks invested in companies that are experiencing high annual gains in their profits. The underlying idea behind a growth stock is a company that grows at a steady rate due to its product or service.

Value stocks

Value stocks are stocks that generally have a low price-to-earnings ratio (P/E defined below). The goal of value managers purchasing value stocks is to find companies whose stocks are currently undervalued—that is, the companies' underlying earnings power is not reflected in their stock prices.

Blend stocks

Blend stocks are stocks that show both growth and value characteristics.

P/E ratio

The Price-Earnings (P/E) ratio is computed by dividing the latest closing price by the latest available earnings per share. The P/E ratio is one of the most widely used measures for evaluating the price of a stock. It has little meaning alone, but when compared with the company's past P/E ratios and with the P/E ratios of similar companies, it becomes a valuable yardstick. Many investors use the P/E ratio of the blue-chip Dow Jones Industrial Average as a standard of comparison. For example, if the DJIA has a P/E ratio of 10 and an individual stock has a P/E ratio of 8, earnings are considered to be underpriced when compared to the market.

Stock tables

"Stock tables summarize the trading activity in individual securities." Stock tables are typically found in financial dailies and, at times, in abbreviated form in local newspapers. Here is an example. Let's take a closer look so you can understand the information you can find here.

52 Weeks				Yld			Vol				Net
Hi	Lo	Stock	Sym	Div	%	PE	100s	Hi	Lo	Close	Chg
28 ½	15 ⅟₁₆	XX Corp	XXC	.34	1.6	13	1350	21 ¹⁵⁄₁₆	20 ½	21 ⅟₁₆	– ⅟₁₆

The first column reports the highest price paid for the stock over the last 52 weeks, excluding the previous day's trading. The second column gives the lowest price paid over the last 52 weeks.

The name of the company issuing the stock is in the third column and its symbol in column four. Column five, labeled "Div," is the annual cash dividend based on the rate of the last quarterly payout. The next column gives the yield percentage, which is determined by dividing the cash dividend by the closing price of the stock. Column 7 is the P/E ratio. Column 8 gives the number of shares traded in each stock, expressed in hundreds of shares (75 means 7,500 shares were traded that day). The final four columns on the right give the high, low and closing prices for the day and the net change from the previous day.

Stock's beta

Beta is a measurement of a stock's volatility in relation to a market index. For instance, the Standard & Poor's 500 Stock Index has been given a beta of 1. Stocks with betas greater than 1 are considered to be more volatile, but also more potentially rewarding, than the S&P 500. Stocks with betas of less than 1 are generally considered less risky and less rewarding than the S&P 500. A fund with a beta of 1.2 should rise 1.2 times as much as the market when the market is rising. On the other hand, when the market is falling, this same stock is expected to fall in value 1.2 times as much as the market as a whole. So how do you use beta to help you make investment decisions? If you are confident the market is rising, you may want to select a high-beta fund. If you feel the market is falling, a low-beta fund may be the smart move. Caution: even the pros can't guarantee a rise or fall of the market. Guessing the market is risky.

"Cap" or capitalization

The total value of a company's outstanding shares of stock.

Net Asset Value (NAV)

The Net Asset Value is the value of one share in a fund.

Mutual fund

"A mutual fund is a pool of commingled funds contributed by a group of investors and managed by professional fund advisors in exchange for a fee." A mutual fund invests in stocks, bonds or other securities. Instead of purchasing a particular stock, you purchase shares in a whole group of stocks. The combined holdings of stocks, bonds or other securities and assets the fund owns are known as its portfolio.

No-load fund

This is a type of mutual fund that doesn't charge a fee when it is initially issued.

Load fund

This is a type of mutual fund that charges a sales fee or commission when the fund is initially issued.

Prospectus

The prospectus is the fund's selling document and contains information about costs, risks, past performance and the fund's investment goals. A fund's prospectus is your most important source of information for any fund you're considering.

Bonds

Bonds are essentially IOUs issued by companies or governments. The issuer agrees to pay back the face value of the bond over a fixed period of time as well as a fixed rate of interest (called a coupon rate) to the bondholder for the duration of the bond. The value of bonds fluctuates according to two main factors: interest rates and the financial health of the issuer. When interest rates rise, the value of the bond falls. If you have to sell the bond before its maturity date, a declining value could be a problem.

UNDERSTANDING INVESTMENT BASICS

Congratulations! You now can listen to *CNN Financial News* with greater understanding. But there's more to living rich in understanding than listening to the news. You need to make some news of your own with a money-smart approach to investing. In the mountains of financial literature describing wise investing and smart thinking, key concepts appeared over and over again. They are here in this section. Soak them up! This is your foundation to thinking rich. Then, as we explore Living Rich Laws #4 to #10, you'll be ready to apply your knowledge.

Time

Time is your best friend—your secret to managing risk, your key to unlocking the magic of compounding—very simply, your best shot at realizing financial freedom when you're retired. Experts say this one financial tool is the most valuable one of all the strategies in all the personal finance books. Chapter 10 will explain exactly why and how time is your best partner for living a financially rich life.

Compounding

Thanks to compound interest, anyone can become a millionaire. Financial experts often use the word *magic* in connection to compounding, and when you look at the difference compounding makes in the growth of your investment, you'll probably agree there's something magical about this phenomenon. Compounding simply means earning interest on your interest—seems like a little thing, but the impact over time is amazing. Here's an example: Your 18-year-old comes to you one day with determination in his eyes and declares that from this day forward he is saving a dollar a day until the day he retires on his 67th birthday. After you've picked yourself up off the floor, you have a decision to make. You could watch him get the jar out and start stuffing his dollar bills in day after day until on his 67th birthday he opens the jar and pulls

out a whopping $17,640. Or you could help him pu
ing to work on his savings and direct him to a mutu
aging 12 percent interest. He keeps the interest he
account in order to earn interest on his interest. Then
birthday, assuming you're taking your *Daily Benefits*™ dietary supplements and are still up for a party, you could help him celebrate
as he looks at his total savings amount in excess of $1 million.
What do you think? Prefer the jar or compounding? Now do you
see the magic?

When stock prices are falling, bond prices tend to rise.
Having bonds in your portfolio, therefore, helps counteract
declines in the value of your stock.

Dollar-cost averaging

This is another cool money trick. Actually, this isn't a trick—
there's no magic involved here. It is merely a matter of consistency. Instead of reacting to guilt once a year when you realize
you've not contributed to your investment account and you
scrape together $1,000 to get into your account, you would invest
a set amount on a regular basis. What difference does it make?
Here's the neat part—when you invest regularly, over time the
average cost of your shares will be less than if you made sporadic
lump-sum investments (unless you lucked into timing the market
perfectly). The fact is, markets do fluctuate. But dollar-cost averaging works because, by being consistent, you're buying more
shares in down markets at cheaper prices. Experts say that in
most cases you'll need a full market cycle (about five years) to get
the full benefit of this strategy. Dollar-cost averaging doesn't

mean you can't lose money or that you can't make money if you invest a lump sum at the beginning of a market rise. It does mean, however, that by taking advantage of it—spreading your dollars out consistently—you are able to sidestep the common mistake of buying high and selling low.

Liquidity

Liquidity refers to how easily you can turn your investment into cash without significant risk of loss. Generally, the safest investments are the most liquid. For example, savings accounts, CDs and Treasury Bills are safe, liquid investments. As a trade-off, they will also provide smaller returns over the long run.

Risk

Risk is the chance you take of making or losing money on your investment. Typically, higher returns require the investor to assume greater risk. To manage away risk, it is smart to diversify by investing in a number of different stocks, bonds and cash investments. (Mutual funds are an ideal way to spread your risk.) To manage away the inflation risk, choose investments with a return rate equal to or above the inflation rate. Also, to manage away risk, give your investments time to overcome short-term stock volatility (more about managing away risks in Chapter 5).

Diversification

Diversification means spreading your investments among different asset classes (stocks, bonds, precious metals, real estate, etc.) instead of investing in only one type of security or mutual fund. You should be sure to round out your portfolio with investments that typically do well under different market conditions.

Asset allocation (balance)

This is different from diversification. Diversification means you own many different stocks or bonds, whereas asset allocation or balance means you carefully mix investment markets or asset classes according to your current age or investment objectives. Chapter 4, Balance It Out, will explain how.

NOW THE SUBPLOT IN THINKING RICH

Now that you're thinking rich on a conscious level, it's time to dig a little deeper and add the power of your subconscious. You have a choice. You can wallow around in self-defeating thoughts and suck the juice out of what could be. Or you can open your heart, open your mind, embrace the possibilities and become all your little-girl daydreams envisioned you to be.

Volumes have been written about the power of positive thinking. With Mary Kay, you've seen it in action in the lives of women all around you. But to live a rich life, you need to do more than appreciate positive thinking. You need to do more than believe in positive thinking. You need to practice it.

LESSON IN THINKING RICH

I use affirmations to stay focused and overcome negative self-talk. I am continually developing my vision of myself and my life. I am sometimes surprised by negative thoughts that pop into my mind about myself. I bring them out in the open and affirm positive things. Every six months—or when I'm in transition or unhappy—I do a "What do I want?" list. I spend quiet time asking the question and writing down everything that comes to mind. This process allows me to find my heart's desires. I then look at what I need to do differently to achieve these desires. I choose what I'm willing to work on and set goals. I then make an affirmation tape to keep me on track. It works!

—SUE YELVINGTON O'NEILL, Independent Sales Director

Which are you—a rich thinker or a poor thinker? Poor thinkers see themselves as victims. Someone is always out to get them. This is a dog-eat-dog world they say, and they have every intention of being the top dog—the ones who do unto others before they do unto them. They waffle through life like willows in a windstorm. Circumstances dictate their choices. They refuse to take responsibility, are full of self-pity, let setbacks stop them and have a reason ready to justify every failure. They cling to their money with tight fists and closed hearts. They believe there isn't enough for everyone so they have to hold on to every penny. They assign motives to others and fail to realize their accusations are merely reflections of their own intentions.

Maybe you've met someone like this. Maybe you live with someone like this. The point is for you to avoid *being* someone like this. To live rich, you must think rich. Here's how:

- Let go of hurts. Carrying around an injustice saps your energy. Emotional baggage left by an unpleasant encounter not only drags you down, it also gets in the way of thoughts that could lift you up. From now on, turn away, smile, forgive and forget.

- Take a look at your past. Did your parents save, own and value self-reliance? Or was your upbringing one of spending, appearances, renting and poor thinking? Think about your original family and your place in it. What were you there to learn? Appreciate the lesson—whatever it is.

- Look for opportunities rather than making excuses.

- Find reasons to be grateful and express your gratitude every day.

- Accept responsibility rather than look for someone or something to blame.

- Open your hands to others with the intent to improve the condition of someone else (more about the abundance this brings in Chapter 8).

- Lift your expectations. Most people don't experience financial success because they don't think higher than they currently live. They have settled for the way it is. They're comfortable and push themselves only when a crisis hits. They always seem to have just enough money to support their current lifestyles. Stretch your mind. Don't think about getting by, think about getting rich.

LESSON IN MAKING A DIFFERENCE

For me, Mary Kay has opened my life to all kinds of women who want growth. I tell everyone I talk to about Mary Kay that my mission as an Independent Sales Director is to create an atmosphere of unconditional love where other women's self-esteem can grow and they can blossom into the women God wants them to be. I'm convinced if you fix a woman's self-esteem, you have fixed her income for life.

— JANET McMULLIN, Independent Sales Director

- Quit connecting money with pain. If spending money on utility bills, taxes, groceries, your mortgage and all your other expenses is a painful experience for you, you are creating a poverty-magnet around every dollar. Here's how. If you believe spending money is painful, your subconscious is whispering that it stands to reason everyone else feels the same way. Consequently, you are obviously causing pain to other people each time you accept money from them. You'll believe that you're damaging them when they spend money with you. Your income, therefore, will be limited to the amount of pain you are willing to cause others. If you believe your expenses hurt you and, in turn, you hurt others when you cause them expense, you won't make more money than you absolutely need. The answer? Stop connecting pain with money. Joyfully write that check to the electric company. Haven't you loved seeing after dark? Every dollar you spend is well deserved. That's the attitude. That's the feeling you need in your heart to feel no hesitation about asking others to spend money with you. Connect joy with paying for what you use and have. The result? You'll watch your income begin to rise right along with the joy you feel in paying others. Try it.

- Understand the difference between happiness and joy. Happiness is situational. If you get the promotion, you feel happy. If you get the man, you feel happy. If you get the new couch, you feel happy. Joy, on the other hand, is soulful. If you don't get the promotion, you still have joy. If you don't get the man, you still have joy. If you don't get the couch, you still have joy. Joy is a relaxed understanding that there's something to be gained from every experience. There is always a better promotion, man, couch to come your way when the time is right. Joy is peace. Joy is the ultimate reward of living rich.

Speak rich

We've examined what goes on in the mind of the rich. Now, what about their words? What is the language of the rich? For example, what do the rich say about debt? Do they say, "I'll never pay this off. If only I could get a break, I would have a better shot at this. I know I should pay on this bill, but I just can't do it!" Think about the person you thought of in Chapter 1 as a person to emulate. Can you imagine that person speaking like this?

Probably not. Rich language doesn't have words like *if only*, *I know I should*, and *can't* in its vocabulary. Words like *if only . . . I would have* is a cop-out phrase. It gives you a way to avoid responsibility. Laying a failure on something that did or did not happen makes avoiding your debt or your lack of saving more comfortable. If your subconscious excuses you from your responsibilities, what will push you out of your comfort zone to make a difference in your life? If your subconscious isn't pushing, it's likely no part of you will be.

Here's another example of poverty language: "I know I should." Have you ever noticed the people who say "should" a lot—"I should do this . . . I should do that"—typically never get around to doing anything? *Should* is another one of those words that absolves us from responsibility. If you say you "should" do something, more than likely you have no real intent of doing it. It just makes you feel more righteous about not doing it. To live rich, substitute *will* for *should*. "I know I will pay this debt." "I know I will build my investment account."

And what about that pesky little word that is a favorite in the language of poverty—that four-letter word, *can't?* Take it out of your vocabulary. Again, *will* is a good substitute. In fact, following the lessons of Mary Kay, put a little rhythm in it and say, "I want. I will. I can do anything!"

The message here is simple. Speak the words you want to be true. Before you say anything about your financial situation, ask yourself if you want what you're about to say to be true. If the answer is "no," then don't speak the words. Thoughts lead to words. Words lead to action. Give yourself every opportunity to achieve your financial goals by speaking only the words you want to see come true. For instance, before you say, "I'll never get around to filling out that mutual-fund application. I know I should, but I can't seem to find the time," ask yourself, "Is this what I want?" Instead of justifying a spending spree with the words, "I can't help it—I just like spending! I'm a shopaholic," ask yourself if this is what you want. Give yourself a chance at changing by saying something like, "I am spending money on the things I can afford to buy." Shifting the way you speak will take discipline, but the results will begin to appear on your balance sheet. Remember the litmus test when you speak about money: "Is this what I want?" Say only what you want to be true. Swallow those "can'ts," "should-haves" and "if onlys." Don't let them out to clutter the airwaves and sabotage your opportunity to live rich.

Interest is the payment you receive for loaning someone money (such as when you buy a bond). Interest is also the fee you pay when you borrow money.

Act rich

There is no shortage of financial advice out there about actions to take with money. Some of it is conflicting and certainly not all strategies for investing are the same. The good news for all of us who have to make sense of this advice in order to act on it is this—there are a few definite do's that consistently appear. Before you formulate your investment action plan, take a look at these key actions suggested by the experts:

DEFINITE DO'S:

1. **Be consistent.** Consistency allows you to take advantage of dollar-cost averaging so you pay on average the best possible price for your stocks. Making disciplined, regular investments over a long period of time is one of the most successful methods of accumulating wealth. And the good news? You don't need a lot of money to execute this "do."

2. **Be appropriate.** This isn't a moral judgment. Being appropriate in your investment strategy means matching your investments to your tolerance level for risk. It also means

matching the mix of your investment types to your changing financial objectives, which typically change as your life stages change (more about this in Chapter 4).

3. **Be patient.** In other words, don't sweat the stock market's ups and downs. Day-to-day volatility is extreme and reacting to these extremes is hazardous to your financial health. According to a study by Terrance Odean, professor of finance at the Graduate School of Management at the University of California at Davis, as seen on www.usnews.com, analysis of some 60,000 discount-brokerage accounts found that traders who were most active netted an average return of just 9.6 percent annually while the benchmark that year (1997) netted 17.1 percent. And according to another study by this same professor and Professor Brad Barber, reported by the *American Funds Investor,* men seem to be more prone to jumping around in fits of trading than women. In this study, men were found to trade stocks 50 percent more often than women. And the results of all this activity? A lower return, according to the study. Men, on average, had a net return that was 1.4 percent lower than the return earned by women. Patience suggested in the "buy and hold" strategy is apparently more natural for women. Not surprised? (There is more about the value of patience in Chapter 5.)

4. **Give your investments time.** Procrastination is your future's biggest threat. Remember the example of the 18-year-old who, by investing a dollar a day, retired with over a million dollars? He gave his dollars time (and, of course, the magic of compounding). Smart!

The word pension *comes from the Old French, meaning* payment.

THE RAINBOW CONNECTION

The best plan of action is to act and then sit back and monitor. Not a complicated concept. To help make this plan even less complicated, Mary Kay has found a program ideal to help with investments. Exclusively for Independent Sales Directors, this program is called The Rainbow Program and is administered by one of the premier mutual fund management companies in the U.S., the Invesco Funds Group.* To make it convenient for you to apply the four "definite do's" suggested by the experts, the Rainbow Program has been created to solve three of your investment objectives: to save for retirement, to save for your children's college education, to save for large expenses before retirement such as a home, a car, or an emergency fund. The program allows you

- to invest a portion of your commission check automatically (consistency),
- to select the investment mix appropriate to your age and objectives (appropriateness),
- to enjoy professional management with a long-term perspective on growth (patience),
- to start immediately (smart!).

Here are your Rainbow options:

- a Simplified Employee Pension plan (SEP) for retirement
- a savings plan to build a fund for whenever you need it
- the "Invesco Baby Bucks" plan specially set up for a minor

For more information, call Invesco at 1-800-835-2323 and get the full story of your options. You also may want to visit the Invesco Web site: www.invesco.com.

---

* Mary Kay Inc. does not endorse Invesco or in any way warrant, represent or guarantee the safety or the rate of return of any investment with Invesco.

Six Most Important Things to Do to Think, Speak and Act Rich

1. Keep learning. Reread the explanation of financial terms and investing concepts in this chapter. Find a stock table in your paper and test your understanding. Listen to financial news on television and say, "Hmmm, interesting," several times during each broadcast. You'll impress your husband and remind yourself to really listen.

2. Go online to financial sites and go exploring. Ask for a daily or weekly financial update of the high points of the national financial news to be e-mailed to you. And remember, whatever you see in the news, take a deep breath and hold steady to your long-term strategy.

3. Kick your subconscious into high gear toward a rich life by expecting more, disconnecting pain from spending money and opening up to others with the intent of improving their lives.

4. Never say "if only," "I can't" or "I should have" when talking about money.

5. Ask yourself before you say anything about your money situation if you want what you're about to say to be true. If you don't, don't say it.

6. Take advantage of the three powerful money tools (compounding, dollar-cost averaging and time) by opening an investment account today and committing to a set investment amount monthly.

Definitions of Living Rich

To be blessed with a personal relationship with God and
to share that with others.
—*Judy Dunlap*

My family's first new car, first "real" vacation and a beautiful
two-story home with a pool. I have started investing for my children's
education and our beautiful future.
—*Joy Tucker*

Having a lifestyle that allows for a personal trainer, a massage
once a week, travel, shopping, doing charity work—doing all the
things I've ever wanted to do!
—*Susan H. Weeks*

Availability to help others and having no worries about the future.
—*Sue H. Flowers*

Living rich really has nothing to do with money.
It just makes it more fun to share.
—*Karen Mosel*

The ability to provide all the spiritual, emotional and financial
needs for me and those close to me.
—*Dian Crane*

Having money to provide all the things my family needs
to live without financial stress.
—*Sherry Hanes*

Being able to give of yourself and enrich the lives of others.
—*Kathy Gannon*

Having more money than month! Being able to give my family
the life they deserve.
—*Melanie Stenge*

Living a Rich Life

CHAPTER FOUR

Law #4: Balance It Out

Don't turn your focus away from what is truly important. Instead, learn to evaluate your success by the balance you achieve in your life.
— MARY KAY ASH

IF YOU LOOK BACK AT YOUR LIST OF VALUES, balance is probably there. You'll also find it mentioned in several of the living-rich definitions throughout this book. We *like* balance—and we're not alone. In a 1994 survey by the U.S. Department of Labor asking over a quarter of a million women the number-one issue they would like brought to the U.S. President's attention, their answer was "the difficulty of balancing work and family obligations." Not everyone has found balance, but you can be sure everyone *wants* it. Mary Kay Ash knew the importance of balance back in 1963 when she based her company on the priority list of God first, family second, career third. Mary Kay knew that time should be divided in a way that allows what you *do* to support and respect who you *are* as well as who you *love*. The result? Perfect balance of your work life, your spiritual life and your family life.

So let's address this issue first—the balancing of your time. Then we'll round out Law #4 by looking at balancing values with consumption, ownership with responsibility and, finally, your investment portfolio with the stages of your life. Juggling is a way of life for women. By practicing Law #4, you'll remember to keep your eyes on the ball, your feet firmly planted and the three areas of your life—spiritual, family and career—perfectly airborne.

Balance time

According to a 1998 survey by the National Partnership for Women & Families, Americans say (by a margin of three to one) that "time pressures on working families" are getting worse, not better, and that "finding time for both work and family responsibilities" is tougher to do now than five years ago. Half of those surveyed personally worry about shortchanging their families, their jobs and themselves because they don't have enough time to do everything they need to do. And to place an even bigger premium on balance, some futurists say the most coveted asset in the next decade will not be material belongings; it will be *time*.

The Priority List—
God first, family second, career third

So how do we make the most of this stuff life is made of—time—so we can juggle our roles with confidence rather than guilt? First, we create a sense of order—not of the chaos, but of our values. As Stephen Covey advises, we schedule our priorities rather than prioritize our schedule. That means devoting time to what is most important in our lives—taking control of time so the big things (our values) aren't squeezed out by the details. God first, family second, career third—that rule of thumb prioritizes the big things. As Mary Kay says, "In that order, everything works. Out of that order, nothing does." And that "nothing" includes your finances. When you're feeling inadequate in important parts of your life, guilt bubbles up, stress builds, and the emotional energy you need to work on your financial goals is tapped out. As a result, instead of realizing security, peace of mind, personal health, spiritual growth and all your other values, you bury yourself in piles of minutiae. The real danger in this priority scramble is the fact that since you feel busy, you delude yourself into thinking you must be going somewhere. You're getting things done! You're important! You're moving and shaking! The fact is you're spinning your wheels—a hubbub of activity going nowhere.

LESSON IN PRIORITIES

*O*ne day at work I received a phone call from the school that my son had been injured. I told my boss I had to go. She didn' t like it, but she let me go. He had injured his ankle while playing football. The next day he injured it again, and again I was called. My boss told me I couldn' t go, but I left anyway and took my son to the hospital for x-rays. The next day my boss told me my job should come first, before my family. That statement helped me make a decision that changed my life forever. I gave her my notice of resignation. That was the day I began working hard on my Mary Kay business. Two months later I had my 100th skin-care customer. I have been blessed not only with the use of three career cars, diamond rings and my confidence back, but also with the fact that my three children have grown up very confident and smart because of the beliefs we have in this Company. I am able to serve my Lord whenever He calls me and to be there for my husband and children. Best of all, I no longer have to answer to anyone when it comes to my children. I can put my priorities in order the way Mary Kay has taught us.

—SUSIE MACIAS, Independent Sales Director

*Balancing tip from Independent National Sales Director
Joan Rector: So you know when to "shut down," hang a sign
saying "Office Closed" on your office door. When my
children were 6, 9, 10 and 11, each had one night a week
to cook dinner and clean up the kitchen.
(The 6-year-old is now a chef!)*

To take a Priority List such as God first, family second and career third off these pages and into your life, you need to systemize your activities. If you don't have a planner, get one. If you do, begin pulling your life and time together in this one place. This is your master calendar—it pictures not only your business appointments, but your spiritual and family commitments as well. Give yourself space for your list of values; your financial goals; a place to track expenses; addresses; important information such as your husband's Social Security number, his shirt and shoe size; your daily journal; your exercise track record. Keep your life in this planner. This way you'll write things down only *one* time. You'll stop running to the family calendar and then back to your business calendar before making appointments. You'll begin to see the big picture and how your life merges in all key areas of success—spiritual, family, career, health, financial and personal.

When your planner includes your *whole* life, you can take a look back at the week and see the balance—or lack of balance. You can check to see if your priorities were scheduled or if the "urgent" took the place of the "important." Create your master calendar and live it for one week before deciding if it works. Then to help you decide, flip back to the next page and rate the balance you see there. Did the time you spend reflect your Priority List?

Checking your balance

Example of One Week's Balancing Act

(The shaded portion represents time spent in each key area.)

	Sun.	M	T	W	Th	F	Sat.
Spiritual	▓			▓			
Family	▓						
Career							
Financial							
Health							

LESSON IN MAKING CHOICES

*O*ne year after I became an Independent Sales Director, my husband and I agreed we wanted our boys to get to know their grandparents better. We chose to move to Minnesota where we grew up. Six weeks later we sold our home. I left 55 Independent Beauty Consultants and 200 customers and my husband resigned from his job. When we moved, my husband went out to find work and I went out to find women to facial! One year later my dad passed away unexpectedly. Because of the move, I had the opportunity to be at his bedside and our boys were able to create several memories with their grandfather. With Mary Kay, we have choices. In our experience we saw how putting God first, our relationships with each other second and our careers third really worked. **—Fern Gerdes, Independent Senior Sales Director**

THE STRESS-BUSTING LIST

The simple truth is this: We all have the same number of hours in a day. It's how effectively we use those hours that determines if we live a rich life—or not. Time management may not seem like a financial issue, but it may be your most important one. Read about time management or enroll in a time-management class. Prioritize, plan and monitor your balance. The point is, you must get a grip on time if you want to live a rich life. Here's a start—time-management gurus suggests these three essentials:

1. **Simplify** In other words, identify your nonessentials and cut them out of your life. Extra stuff means more stuff to insure, fix, clean, move or store. Give away what you don't need. Not only will you simplify your life by decluttering it, you'll also give back value to the items you don't use—a sure sign of respect for money. Clean out your drawers, throw away the junk, give away the unnecessary and rediscover the missing. If you want to live rich, you need to truly appreciate what you own and respect your money by valuing its purchases. Stuffing clothes in the attic or piling old books in a closet is disrespectful of the money used to purchase these things in the first place. Respect your money, value what you have—whether in the hands of someone else who needs it or in your own hands. In the process you'll rediscover time you'd been wasting plowing through the clutter. Use that time to balance out your personal life, your family life and your financial life—spend it on a hot bath, take a walk with your husband, read *The Wall Street Journal*, lie on the floor with your kids and play Tickle-Monster, balance your checkbook, read an inspirational book or just do nothing at all. The point is this—by getting rid of the stuff you *don't* need you'll have time for the stuff you *do*.

2. **Delegate** After you've decluttered your life, you're surrounded by the essentials, which require a different approach to erasing

stress and adding time. This step involves rounding up rein-
forcements and dividing up the details. To enlist the family in
this delegation phase of your balancing act, family counselors
suggest you call a family meeting and ask for help redistribut-
ing the jobs around the house. Make a list and ask for volunteers. After assignments have been cheerfully snapped up (in a
Ward-and-June-Cleaver kind of way), be sure to get specific
about all aspects of each job—your
expectations of quality, the fre-
quency of the job, the supplies to
be used, the accountability issues.
Create a visual reminder of delegation details and post it on your
refrigerator. Expect complete coop-
eration and hold everyone accountable (more about getting your family involved in your *rich life* in
Chapter 7).

> *According to many
> financial advisers,
> everyone should hold
> some stocks, even a
> conservative 80-year-
> old couple.*

3. **Systemize** Only when you've created free time by simplifying
and delegating will you be able to increase your productivity
toward achieving any goal—financial or otherwise. To help you
along, here's one more tip the time management experts suggest—create systems for life's *routine* things so you have time
for the truly *important* ones. Creating a master calendar and
having a planner with everything you need in one place is a
great start. Organizing your financial documents and having a
filing system will shave off more minutes from the routine to
be applied to the important. Are there other systems you
could put into place? How about a set time for making calls, a
block of time you don't take calls, a year's supply of birthday
cards stacked in the order you'll mail them, the due dates for
bills posted on your master calendar? Anything you can put on
a no-brainer kind of systems track, do so. The more minutes
you free, the greater balance you achieve.

> ## LESSON IN SYSTEMATIZING
>
> *I knew I only wanted to work four days a week when I started my Mary Kay business and that's exactly what I've always done. When I work, I'm focused and very concise about the activity. I respect my work time. Knowing my purpose and what I want from my business has helped me set boundaries. We adopted a baby girl last November. In the 13 months we've had her, I've been able to adjust my business to always be there for her. Working from home is the greatest luxury, but it's also the greatest responsibility. I determined I would work four days a week and get help to support me in areas that are a challenge to me. I have a consistent system of goal-setting—every month before the month is over, I think about what we will accomplish the next month. The biggest lesson I've learned in keeping a handle on my schedule is to keep my purpose clearly in sight. I had to learn to say no, not to dally on the phone and eliminate the things that have to be done that drain my energy. When you do the things that make you feel good and delegate the rest, you don't get drained.*
>
> — **DEBRA WEHRER**, Independent Senior Sales Director

Balance values with consumption

THE FLOW OF FOCUS

If you pull together the essence of Mary Kay's teachings and apply that essence to the way you treat money, you'll notice a flow of focus that automatically balances your values with your spending patterns or consumption. Remember her Priority List? God first, family second, career third? The top two priorities on this list involve focusing on your relationships—with God and with your family. A second foundational pillar of Mary Kay's philosophies is the Golden Rule, another principle that suggests focusing on others—on relationships. What does this have to do with spending patterns? Think about it. If you place your relationships first, then obviously those relationships will be first in dictating your spending decisions. Those things that support your spiritual life and your loved ones or were created *from* love or *for* love should take precedence over everything else if you want to balance your values with consumption.

After supporting relationships, Mary Kay's teachings point to the practical—she's a woman, after all—she understands the realities of life. You may have read one of her favorite sayings, "From birth to 14 a woman needs good parents and good health. From 14 to 40 she needs good looks. From 40 to 60 she needs personality. From 60 on she needs cash."

So, after supporting relationships, your focus to dictate spending decisions should shift to accumulating cash. You don't see on Mary Kay's list of needs anything about a trendy wardrobe, a big house or snazzy jewelry. The bottom line here is "cash." So if watching your investment accounts increase in value each month becomes more rewarding to you than picking up the latest and hottest new gizmo, then you know your focus is on track—you value the accumulation of cash more than things. To create a life of financial freedom, this shift in the order of money and things needs to take place. Sure, it's more fun to look in the mirror at a new pair of drop-dead gorgeous shoes than it is to invest the $75 it took to get those shoes. But which do you value more—that moment of fun in the mirror or a future of financial freedom? Your answer suggests your flow of focus. Keep in mind, Mary Kay taught us that "you can never obtain riches until you begin to enrich the lives of others." In other words, relationships come first. Then she taught us to get practical—value money before things. (Mary Kay was a champ at clipping coupons!) So follow her lead, balance your values with consumption by keeping your focus in this order: 1) relationships, 2) cash, 3) stuff (more about making "rich" spending decisions in Chapter 6).

Balance ownership with responsibility

People who spend their lives studying the ups and downs and ins and outs of money tend to think of money as a magnetized force that's attracted to certain behaviors and repelled by others. Pennies vacuumed into dust bags, dollar bills crumpled up in pockets, financial papers scattered in drawers and on desk tops indicate an attitude about money that leads to waste and neglect and missed opportunities for growth. On the other hand, money that is nurtured indicates an attitude that leads to duplication and wealth. In other words, ownership balanced with responsibility creates greater rewards.

Remember the parable of the "talents" in the New Testament? A "talent" referred to a rather large sum of money. One man was given one talent. Instead of using it, sharing it or making it grow, he buried it. So it was taken away. Another man was given two talents, which he turned into two more. For his responsible use of his talents, he was rewarded two additional talents. And a third man was given five talents. When he doubled his five, he was given five more—*plus* the talent of the first man who lost his. The financial lesson we can take from this parable has to do with the responsibility that comes with ownership and the growth that responsibility allows. Being responsible with what you're given may mean investing wisely or spending wisely—or it may simply mean getting organized. We'll cover investing and spending in Chapters 5 and 6, so let's focus now on getting organized.

Organizing, listing and filing

Remember, systemizing is one of the top three essentials to saving time. This section about organizing your financial documents will not only help you be more responsible toward your money in order to attract more of it, it will also help protect your time.

1. **Financial experts agree that the first step is to set up a filing system that includes the following categories:**

   - bank statements (keep canceled checks for at least three years)
   - creditors (how to set up this file is included in Chapter 9)
   - insurance (keep policies here including car, health, life, rental or homeowner's)
   - an inventory of things you own and records of major purchases
   - investment account statements (include pension plan or retirement plan statements and mutual fund and other investment account statements)
   - medical bills
   - monthly expenses (rent, telephone, utilities, etc.)
   - mortgage information
   - receipts (write dates, locations and business purposes on each receipt)
   - tax returns (maintain at least seven years and file with each return your W-2 forms, income statements from your bank and investment accounts, canceled checks for deductible expenditures)
   - your will (if your filing system is a fireproof box)

Tip: Make this filing system a fireproof box and give yourself additional peace of mind. Or consider a safe-deposit box for documents such as birth, marriage and death certificates, divorce or separation agreements, title papers to real estate or other assets, mortgage papers, stock certificates, photographs or videotapes of the inside and outside of your home for insurance purposes. Make copies of all your printed records for easy reference before you place them in the box. Make sure someone knows the location of your safe-deposit box and the keys. Be sure to keep your will somewhere else—at your attorney's office or in your fire-proof box at home. Safe-deposit boxes are sealed at death until the IRS sees what's inside. This could prevent your will from being read for some time after your death.

2. **Keep accurate records in your check register.** When you write a check, write it in your check register immediately. If you use a debit card, write the amount in your register immediately. Keep your checkbook up to the minute. And, of course, when your bank statement comes in, balance your register.

3. **Keep your financial goals in front of you.** Write your financial goals—the ones you created in Chapter 2—in your planner. Attach the target date to each specific goal. Write your purpose for each goal beside that goal. Jot down the immediate actions you must take to meet each goal. Keep this "goal file" up to date and in clear view.

Balance your portfolio with your life

Risk tolerance is how much risk you're willing to take in order to increase the level of potential reward. Risk and reward go hand-in-hand.

This portion of your balancing act has clear financial repercussions. You have two primary considerations when balancing your investment portfolio with your life—the first one is your risk tolerance and the second is your age and the financial objectives that go along with it. Bill Griffeth, business journalist on CNBC and author of the book *10 Steps to Financial Prosperity*, identified four levels of risk and the types of investments represented in each one. Before you determine your comfort level for risk in order to start balancing your portfolio, here is a full view of the sliding scale:[1]

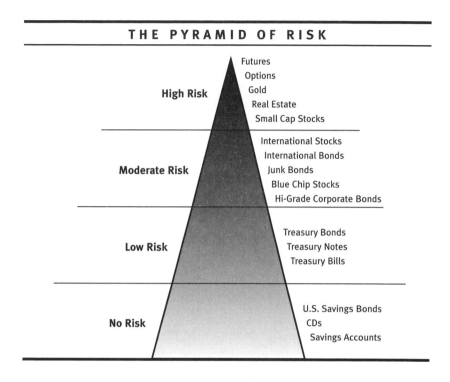

THE PYRAMID OF RISK

High Risk
Futures
Options
Gold
Real Estate
Small Cap Stocks

Moderate Risk
International Stocks
International Bonds
Junk Bonds
Blue Chip Stocks
Hi-Grade Corporate Bonds

Low Risk
Treasury Bonds
Treasury Notes
Treasury Bills

No Risk
U.S. Savings Bonds
CDs
Savings Accounts

Griffeth contends that a successful portfolio should include investments from each of the four risk categories—how you balance them will be determined by your age and your personal comfort level for risk. You may be thinking that if given a choice, the low-risk category certainly sounds a whole lot more comfortable. But you have to remember, the lower the risk, the lower the potential for return. And the lower the return, the greater the chance that inflation will eat away at the value of your investment, ultimately making the no-risk investment one of the riskiest. Just trying to keep you alert. The reality is there's *always* risk—it may come in the form of stock volatility that threatens short-term market investments, inflation that threatens the value of savings accounts or increasing interest rates that drive down

*The later you start
investing, the less risk
you can afford to take.*

the value of bonds. Dealing with risk is a way of life in the financial world, so here's the trick—understand it's there, decide your tolerance for it, and balance your portfolio with that knowledge in mind.

To help you with your balancing act, take a look at these three investment styles suggested by Griffeth in his book.[2] Which one seems to fit you?

1. The "speculator" is comfortable with risk, in fact actually seeks it out in order to make short-term gains (that's the *hope*). Speculators have a Rambo-esque quality about their style— they head out full-speed ahead right to the top of the risk barometer. Financial experts say there's a time for this high-risk style. For instance, when you're young and have plenty of time to ride out the highs and lows of the market, you may want to try a little Rambo investing.

2. The "investor" is willing to assume some risk in order to create a higher return than a savings account could, but isn't quite so Rambo-like as the speculator. The investor in this mid-range of risk tolerance is more like Indiana Jones—cautiously opti-mistic. You need a little Indiana Jones in your portfolio when

*Historically, stocks have been very volatile over short periods
but have performed well over 10- to 20-year time-frames.
Risk declines as the time-frame increases—a key concept in asset
allocation (balancing your portfolio with your age and objectives).*

you are in your 30s and 40s and have time to allow retirement money to grow.

3. The "saver" is the third investment style. The saver's main goal is to preserve every cent of principal by avoiding as much obvious risk as possible. Savers have a Huckleberry Hound kind of approach going on—sitting still with their eyes on the mound of earth where they buried that bone. Savers concentrate on the lower part of the risk barometer. This style is appropriate for money you're saving for a short-term goal, such as a downpayment for a house or a remodeling job in your kitchen or on your face.

According to the experts, smart investors should be a little of all three—Rambo, Indiana Jones and Huckleberry Hound—depending on their ages and financial objectives. Here are financial journalist Bill Griffeth's suggestions to balance your portfolio with your age and your tolerance for risk:[3]

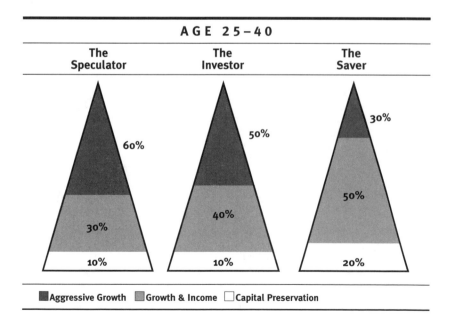

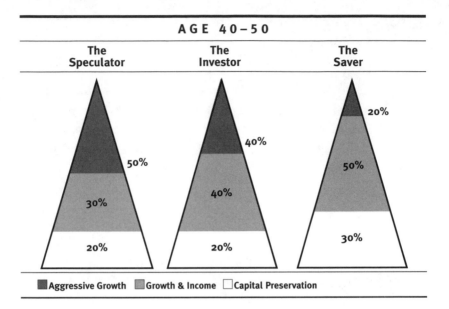

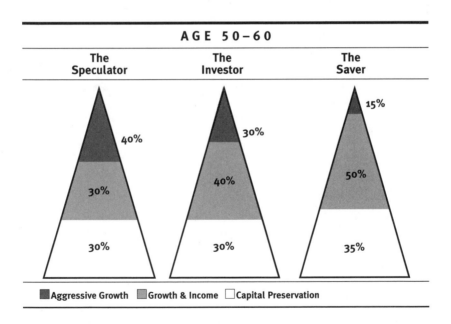

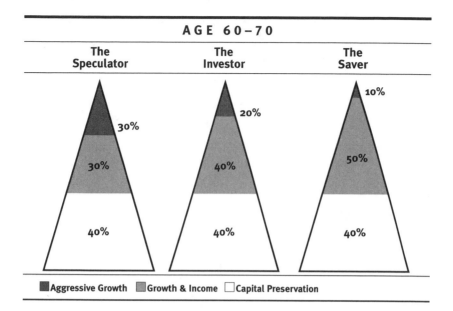

AGE 60–70

The Speculator — The Investor — The Saver

Aggressive Growth · Growth & Income · Capital Preservation

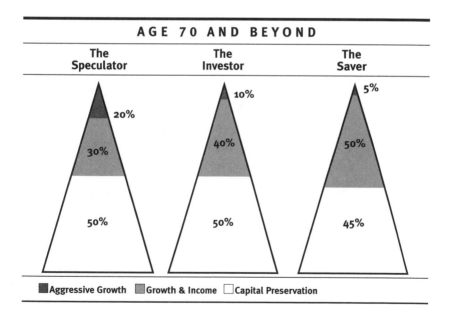

AGE 70 AND BEYOND

The Speculator — The Investor — The Saver

Aggressive Growth · Growth & Income · Capital Preservation

Balancing your portfolio with your life by spreading out your investments over various investment categories is smart for a lot of reasons. The Women's Institute for a Secure Retirement lists the following:[4]

- Predicting which type of investment will do best in any given year is practically impossible. (All financial sources were unanimous in their discouragement of trying to time the market.)

- Some years bonds have the best returns.

- Stocks, however, have historically the strongest record of high returns over the long run.

- Cash typically provides the lowest return but the greatest liquidity (CDs, money-market funds, savings accounts, Treasury Bills).

According to Henry S. Brock, the *Financial Analyst Journal* stated almost all (93 percent) of a portfolio's success depends on asset allocation—simply, the balancing of your investments over various categories to fit specific life stages or objectives. Very little success (7 percent) depends on the selection of individual stocks, bonds or mutual funds.[5]

According to Edward T. Koch and Debra DeSalvo, some 60 million Americans directly own common stocks listed on the New York Stock Exchange, while 130 million own shares indirectly through mutual funds.

THE COMPLETE IDIOT'S GUIDE TO INVESTING LIKE A PRO,
E. KOCH AND D. DESALVO, ALPHA BOOKS, 1999.

Six Most Important Things to Do to Balance It Out

1. Create a master calendar and schedule your priorities.

2. Get a grip on time by simplifying, delegating and systematizing.

3. Balance your values with consumption by focusing on relationships first, cash second and stuff third.

4. Organize your financial documents into the categories listed on page 73 and file them in a fireproof box.

5. Find your age and risk-tolerance level on pages 77–79. Balance your investment portfolio accordingly.

6. Check with a financial adviser for additional help in balancing your accounts appropriate to your age, tolerance for risk and financial objectives.

Definitions of Living Rich

A beautiful home, an office in the home "to die for,"
and the flexibility to do for my family while earning
a great income.
—*Doris M. Spells*

Being happy every day you wake up.
—*Jackie I. Burden*

Being debt-free and living in the home of my dreams.
—*Marge Heard*

I am rich with self-esteem and self-confidence.
—*Sonya Coleman*

Living rich is feeling content with the choices I make.
—*Lori Mueller*

Having a nice-sized retirement fund.
—*Deborah Robina*

Being at peace with myself, my family and my God.
—*Susan Garmon*

Not having money determine my decisions.
—*Gina Gildone*

Having my faith, family and career in balance.
—*Lisa Bonadonna Madden*

Being financially free and having time with my family.
—*Sonya Dudley*

Balance.
—*Karen Saphos*

Living a Rich Life

CHAPTER FIVE

Law #5: Take the Long-term Look

*If you do the things you ought to do when you ought to do them,
then someday you can do the things you want to do when you want
to do them.* —MARY KAY ASH

AGAIN, MARY KAY WAS RIGHT ON TARGET when it comes to living
a financially rich life. In fact, investment experts say the single
most important thing you could do to secure wealth is to have a
long-term perspective. Even when you can't see down the road
to your destination, understanding that what you do today will
determine where you are tomorrow is the key to realizing financial goals. It's like the cliff diver who watches the ocean below
build and recede and then times his jump so that he actually
leaves the cliff when the ocean goes out and the rocks are fully
exposed beneath him. By the time he hits the water, the ocean
has returned and his entry is safe and beautiful. That takes guts.
It takes faith. It takes understanding that what you do at the
moment determines how you'll fare in the future.

The objective of this chapter is to give you that same kind of
long-term perspective so when you jump into planning your
future, the end result will be exactly as you imagined it to be—

safe and beautiful. Of course, this chapter deals only with the knowledge you'll need to plan your future. You'll have to supply the guts and faith to jump in and get started. But with your Mary Kay heritage, courage and faith should come naturally.

So let's expand on the five long-term goals, which we identified in Chapter 1:

1. free-and-clear home ownership
2. college educations for your children
3. million-dollar nest-egg for you
4. a life that realizes your purpose
5. a legacy of security for your heirs

Now let's elaborate on these major goals and apply the wisdom and advice of other financial experts so you'll find yourself in safe waters when the time is right for each one of these goals.

Goal #1: free-and-clear home ownership

More than likely your home is the biggest purchase you'll make in your lifetime. Figuring how much of a home you can afford and how to save the downpayment will be covered in Chapter 6 when we look at budgeting and managing cash flow. For now, let's assume you already have a mortgage so our challenge here is one of focus. We need to take our eyes off the month-to-month for a moment and shift to the big nut—the overall loan amount. That's when you'll begin to see how to put real meaning in the "own" part of home ownership.

When do you want to have your mortgage-burning party? How many years is that from today? It's smart to end your mortgage payments by the time you begin your retirement. The biggest reason is obvious. At best your income is typically reduced by 30 to 50 percent when you retire. If you haven't built

*Too much time on the weekend to worry about
the ups and downs of the stock market seems to be a
dangerous thing—Mondays are historically the biggest down
days in stocks. The key to making money in stocks is to
not get scared out of them.*

an adequate retirement fund, it will drop much more than that. So why would you want to be saddled with the largest monthly payment you have at a time like that?

I know I'm stating the obvious, but only to those with a long-term perspective. So humor me until I get everyone on board. What if you're 45 when you sign your name on that brand-new 30-year mortgage? You have about 20 years to pay it off if you want to retire home-free at 65. What if you're 50 when the clock starts ticking on that 30-year term? Don't look at that monthly payment and say, "I'm fine. We qualified. We can handle this." Instead, look at your mortgage-burning goal. If your goal is to have your mortgage-burning party at age 65, you have 15 years left. The point is, every time you buy a home, the 30-year term gets extended on the bank's calendar; however, if you want to live home-free at retirement, you shouldn't let it get extended on yours. The burn date is the burn date, no matter when the mortgage began or when it's scheduled to end.

If you're still playing around in a month-to-month mentality, let me give you a couple more reasons to shift into big-picture thinking. By paying more each month than you have to, you will do wonders at building your equity (the amount between what you owe and the market value of your home). Take a look at this:

EQUITY ACCUMULATION[1]

($100,000 30-year fixed-rate mortgage with a 7-percent interest rate)

	After five years	After ten years
15-year mortgage	$22,587	$54,607
30-year mortgage	$5,868	$14,187

---

*Choosing the 30-year mortgage over the 15-year mortgage
is OK if you truly have the discipline to invest
the difference between the 30-year payment and what you
would have had to pay monthly on the 15-year mortgage.
If you spend that extra few hundred dollars rather than
put it in a retirement account, it's wiser to choose the
15-year mortgage.*

Even if the home you live in now isn't the home you plan to own during retirement, think of the difference you could make on a downpayment for that ultimate home if you accumulated this kind of accelerated equity in your current home. In this example, in just five years by adding an extra $233.52 a month toward the principal beyond your normal monthly payment, an additional $16,719 in equity was added to the homeowner's side of the ledger. Nice boost to paying down the next home loan.

A third reason long-term thinking is smart when it comes to your mortgage: you'll save oodles of money on interest. For example, on a $150,000 loan at 9-percent interest, over 30 years, you would pay $434,494.80. With a 15-year loan, you would pay $273,850.00—$160,000 less in pure interest. (The monthly payment difference would be roughly $300.) You would save more than the original cost of the home itself by bumping up your payments each month by about 25 percent.

Here's the neat part about all this. You don't have to refinance a current 30-year loan or start out with a 15-year mortgage to get the benefits of one. You can accelerate your equity and slash your interest payments by designing your own "burn my mortgage" program. Here are a couple of suggestions that were adapted from those originally made by CNBC business journalist Bill Griffeth:[2]

Many early American homes placed knobs in the top of the second-story banister to signify the home was owned free and clear. Some folks even hollowed out a spot on the banister and inserted the paid-off mortgage. Where will you put yours?

1. "Make an extra principal payment each month." Your lender will be able to tell you the exact breakdown of principal and interest in your monthly payment if it's not already listed on your payment coupon. Be sure to write a separate check for this principal amount and label the check "principal only." This extra principal payment each month will cut a 30-year mortgage commitment into a 15-year one using your own self-designed plan.

2 "Make an extra mortgage payment each year." If you want to play catch-up this year since you haven't been making the extra principal payments monthly, make an extra monthly payment for the year. Mark that 13th mortgage payment "principal only." The good news? This one extra payment each year will cut a 30-year mortgage down to about a 22-year mortgage. Again, your equity will accelerate; your total interest payment will drop.

Other ways to accomplish the big burn on your retirement date

What if you can't stay in your home the 15 or 30 years to pay off your mortgage, but you still would like to live mortgage-free in retirement? Some financial experts give this advice: pay off half the mortgage, sell your home and buy a condo or townhouse for half the price of your former home. The house is different, but the home-free result is the same. Before you opt for this choice, check with your tax adviser to make sure it's appropriate for your situation.

Here's another angle

If you have the discipline to take the same amount of money it would take each month to prepay your mortgage and invest that amount in your tax-deferred retirement account, this may be your best option. You get the tax advantages of the mortgage interest as well as the tax deduction now on the amount you invest in your account *and* the benefit of compound interest while it's there. With the additional retirement savings, you could use that money to pay off your mortgage sooner. Investigate all your options. The big message here is to remember your burn date and to make it a reality by sticking to the plan you like best.

According to a 1998 AARP survey with Roper Starch Worldwide, 80 percent of baby boomers think they're going to keep working after they turn 65. The reality? They probably won't—only 12 percent of people over 65 hold jobs today.

WWW.RESEARCH.AARP.ORG/ECON/BOOMER

LESSON IN FREE-AND-CLEAR HOME OWNERSHIP

When we originally bought our home we had a $90,000 loan left after our downpayment, which we financed for 30 years with an adjustable interest rate. After three years the interest rate raised our payment almost $300 a month. That's when we decided to get in control of this payment rather than it being controlled by someone else. We sold another property we had and refinanced our mortgage, putting money down on the loan and refinancing it for 15 years. Then we sat down and budgeted our expenses and agreed on an amount we would both pay into our family account. We put an extra $300 to $400 a month in this account to use to pay off our house loan. We made one more principal payment every month. We had taken our first mortgage in 1987. Then in 1990 we refinanced. Five years later we had paid off our home entirely. Not making a house payment afforded us the opportunity to really focus on becoming debt-free—which we did. We have no debt at all. We have only two credit cards—one for personal use and one for business. I found that once you live without the extra money and act like you never have it, then you don't have to have it. Then you're able to put more money toward investments. We're right on track for where we need to be for retirement. We work well within the parameters we've set for ourselves. Living as we do requires a mindset that anybody can develop. It starts with making a decision that you want to be debt-free. Then you need to come up with a plan that you and your husband can agree upon. The peace of mind that you feel when you're not spending tomorrow's dollars on today's purchases is incredible. Being in debt causes stress. We love the feeling we have. Not having a mortgage is such a blessing!

—MARLA BOLLING, Independent Senior Sales Director

Goal #2: College educations for your children

I love Abraham Lincoln's take on the future. He said, "The best thing about the future is that it only comes one day at a time." What a relief! We can take this "future" business in bite-sized

Advisers say the biggest financial error new parents tend to make is to put saving for their children's education over their own retirement security. Instead, of the 10 percent you save from your salary, invest 2 percent of it in college funds and 8 percent for retirement.

chunks. For instance, the day you bring home that precious little goo-goo baby sweetheart from the hospital you have approximately 6,570 days till your bubbly little baby bundle turns into a hormones-gone-amok 18-year-old taking SAT tests and looking through college brochures for cool campuses. So what do you do with those 6,570 days between these two life events?

First, you get out your wallet—you knew that was coming—then you pull out a couple of bucks a day until you have 60 of them by the end of the month. Next, you invest those 60 dollar bills in an investment fund. Then 6,570 days later, you stand before your bubbly little baby bundle (now that he/she is going away, your perception has reverted), and you say, "Sweetheart, you're on your way. Don't worry about the money. Your job is to learn. My job was to help you get started. And I did—$45,471.64 worth of getting started. So take off . . . learn . . . become . . . enjoy . . . and remember—I'll love you forever . . . I'll like you for always. . . ."

Just thinking about that feels great, doesn't it? So break this goal down into one-day increments and make it happen. By investing $60 a month ($2 a day) in an investment fund averaging a 12-percent return compounded monthly, for a period of around 18 years, you can create this warm $45,471.64 off-to-college experience.

Value of college education

And here's the great news—not only will it feel good to send your child to college, the college experience will pay off many times over in the long run. According to a 1994 U.S. Census Bureau report, a high school graduate earns an average of $20,500 whereas a college graduate earns an average of $35,000 a year—73 percent more. That's the value of a college education.

Investment options

There are many plans that will help you turn this long-term goal of college education into a day-by-day reality. Here are a few suggested by Invesco:*

1. **Uniform Gifts/Transfers to Minor Act (UGMA).** You can open an account under your state's UGMA in any one of Invesco's mutual funds. The account is set up in your child's name but is managed by you until the child is 18. At least a portion of the earnings in this account can be taxed at the child's income-tax rate—depending on the child's age and the amount of earnings each year. This tax break makes a UGMA account an attractive way to save for college for parents whose incomes or assets make them ineligible for financial aid.

2. **Education IRA.** Although called an IRA (Individual Retirement Account), an Education IRA has nothing to do with retirement. This is a separate IRA account set up for a named beneficiary for the purpose of funding higher education. The earnings on the account accumulate on a tax-deferred basis and withdrawals for qualified educational purposes are tax-free. There are some income limitations to the Education IRA, which begin at $150,000 for married taxpayers filing jointly and $95,000 for single taxpayers. There is also a ceiling of

---

* Mary Kay Inc. does not endorse Invesco or in any way warrant, represent or guarantee the safety or the rate of return of any investment with Invesco.

annual contributions of $500 per child until the age of 18. Fortunately, you may set up this account in conjunction with a UGMA.

3. **IRS withdrawal.** Beginning in 1998, you could withdraw money from your traditional IRA to help pay college expenses for your child without early distribution penalties.

4. **Regular account.** You have other options in a variety of investment funds. You may want to call Invesco* to discuss which type of account or combination of accounts would be best for you.

College costs

Now here's the bad news—college is expensive and the cost continues to grow at a rate that outpaces inflation—in most years twice the rate of inflation. Here's a snapshot taken for the year 1999: According to the College Board, a public school for an in-state student is roughly $8,000 to $10,000 per year in expenses. For out-of-staters, expect to add approximately $3,000 to that figure. For a private four-year college the number jumps to around $21,000 to $24,000. To help you look ahead to the year your children will enroll, here's a handy chart of projected costs from the College Board:[3]

A good habit to form the day your child is born is to stash all cash gifts your child receives from relatives into their educational funds.

---

* Mary Kay Inc. does not endorse Invesco or in any way warrant, represent or guarantee the safety or the rate of return of any investment with Invesco.

PROJECTED COLLEGE COSTS

Your Child's Freshman Year	Four Years at a Public College	Four Years at a Private College
1994	$34,248	$71,384
1995	$36,645	$76,381
1996	$39,210	$81,727
1997	$41,955	$87,448
1998	$44,892	$93,570
1999	$48,034	$100,120
2000	$51,397	$107,128
2001	$54,994	$114,627
2002	$58,844	$122,651
2003	$62,963	$131,236
2004	$67,371	$140,423
2005	$72,087	$150,252
2006	$77,133	$160,770
2007	$82,532	$172,024
2008	$88,309	$184,066
2009	$94,491	$196,950
2010	$101,105	$210,737
2011	$108,183	$225,489
2012	$115,755	$241,273
2013	$123,859	$258,162
2014	$132,529	$276,233
2015	$141,806	$295,570
2016	$151,732	$316,260
2017	$162,353	$338,398

Source: The College Board 1993–94 Survey

(This chart is based on the College Board's figures for 1993–94 and assumes a 7-percent annual increase. The annual increase between 1982 and 1992 was 7 percent; however, the tuition climb slowed to rise just under 5 percent for the '98–'99 school year.)

If you would prefer taking another look at projections using your children's ages, go to www.invesco.com* to the college funding link and calculate costs for your specific situation.

---

* Mary Kay Inc. does not endorse Invesco or in any way warrant, represent or guarantee the safety or the rate of return of any investment with Invesco.

Other options

I know you're reeling from these figures. I did too. And if you were too busy worrying about diapers and baby food recalls to think about college investing when you brought your little one home, the sticker-shock of a college education and the lack of time you have to build that fund has probably left you feeling a little empty. But cheer up, there's good news. You have options. According to Patrick Callan, who heads the National Center for Public Policy on Higher Education in San Jose, California, and was quoted on the ABC News Web site, total student aid has risen 85 percent since a decade ago. Loans, scholarships and grants for 1998-99 added up to $64 billion.[4]

So how do you tap into some of that for your child? Everything you ever wanted to know and then some about federal financial aid options is in a booklet published by the Department of Education called *The Student Guide.* You may also request a copy from the Federal Student Aid Information Center at this toll-free number: 1-800-4-FED-AID (1-800-433-3243). The high school guidance counselor is also a good source of information, along with the financial aid officer at the college your child plans to attend. A gold mine of information about available scholarships, calculating college expenses, and loans is as close as the Internet. Just type in "college financial aid" and you'll be amazed at the information you'll have before you. If you have a child entering high school, it's not too early to begin your research.

Advisers say to begin the actual planning for financial aid at the beginning of your child's junior year in high school. You won't begin working on the FAFSA (Free Application for Federal Student Aid) until after January 1 of your child's senior year in high school, but you'll be asked to report your income for the previous year. That's why it's smart to work with a financial adviser at the beginning of this year to make sure you make smart money decisions so this snapshot of your income to determine financial aid eligibility is an accurate one. The FAFSA is the federal government's standard form used to determine a student's eligibility for government grants, work-study programs, federally subsidized loans and, in most cases, state grants. You will file this form with the Department of Education. You will then be informed of your expected family contribution in a Student Aid Report sent to you as well as to all the colleges you listed on the FAFSA form.

Also, be sure to check with the financial officer at the college your child plans to attend because many schools require additional forms to be completed. Ask this financial officer what percent of your demonstrated need will be met and how the college determines who gets aid.

And, as one of the best options of all, get your child involved in the planning and payment process. This could be your child's first step toward self-responsibility. Have a family discussion and get your child's take on what is the right balance of parental contributions, scholarships, loans, grants, savings from a summer job and work-study options. Who knows, this may be the perfect bridge to a deeper conversation about "achieving and believing and paying the price."

To bring the concept of college to life during your conversation, you may want to hand your child the ultimate shopping-for-college reference guide, *The College Handbook*, published by the College Entrance Examination Board. This guide profiles over 3,000 colleges—a great way to make the dream come alive!

Tip: To accumulate wealth, practice the fundamentals: Get invested. Stay invested. Reinvest the dividends over time.

LESSON IN FINANCING COLLEGE

Helping my children through college was one of my main motivations for becoming an Independent Sales Director in 1980. We have five children, and we hadn't been able to save a dime toward their education. My husband and I weren't able to attend college, so we were determined that our children would have the opportunity we didn't. Drawing from the philosophy I had learned from Mary Kay, we never talked about "if" they went to college, only "where" they would go and what they would study. I am so grateful to be able to say that because of Mary Kay, those five children collectively have 33 years of college under their belts! I didn't pay every dime because I believe they needed to learn the same work ethic their dad and I have learned. But without Mary Kay, college for them just wouldn't have happened.

— **DONNA WARNOCK,** Independent Senior Sales Director

Goal #3: Million-dollar retirement for you

How does that sound? Do you think of yourself as a millionaire? To become one, you need to start right here, right now getting into a millionaire state of mind. You can *do* this! Practice saying, "I'm a millionaire." Go ahead. Say the word a few times—millionaire, millionaire, millionaire. That word needs to roll right off your tongue as easily as "What's for dinner?" rolls off your husband's. You need to see yourself as 100 percent capable of achieving millionaire status and deserving of every penny of it. You are worth a million bucks. When you believe this and become completely comfortable with this concept—not only wanting it, but fully *expecting* it—then you have a great shot at making it happen.

Remember the 18-year-old who invested $30 a month in an account earning 12-percent return? At age 67, a millionaire was born! Don't have quite that much time? That's OK; you can still do it. Let's say you've hit 30 and you want to get serious about that million-dollar goal. You make more than that 18-year-old, so instead of a buck a day toward savings, you slip into your account five bucks a day. At the end of the month you have $150 to invest. You sock that away, making your total annual investment $1,800. Over the next 37 years, assuming a 12-percent return (quite doable), that $150-a-month habit will turn you into a millionaire—$1,228,887.83 to be exact—on your 67th birthday. This millionaire formula requires time, consistency, a 12-percent growth fund return and a $150-a-month commitment.

A challenge, but doable. Now that we have this million-dollar goal in our minds as achievable, let's examine a few retirement issues to help with the practical steps toward getting there. Advisers say that to prepare for retirement, you need to do three things:

1. assess what you have;
2. determine what you'll need;
3. create an action plan to get you there.

STEP ONE: ASSESS WHAT YOU HAVE

We'll begin this look by examining what we have collectively—as a society. According to the National Commission on Retirement Policy, here are the facts shaping the retirement outlook for Americans:

- **Fact:** We're growing older. In 1950, 7.9 percent of the population was over 65. By 2010, that number will grow to 19.4 percent.

- **Fact:** We're living longer. When Social Security was enacted in 1935, the life expectancy for Americans was under 65 years of age. Based on the 1996 Life Tables produced by the National Center for Health Statistics, 67 percent of females turning 65 by 1996 can expect to live to be 84 years old (i.e., 19 years in retirement).

- **Fact:** More than half of all women 65 or older are widowed, divorced or never married. On average, these older women rely on Social Security for 72 percent of their income. And one in four relies on Social Security for all her income.

- **Fact:** Americans aren't saving as they once did. Their personal saving rate, over 11 percent in 1965, fell into the negative territory by 1999 to –0.7 percent. Half of American families have below $1,000 in net financial savings.

- **Fact:** Social Security is a "pay-as-you-go" system in which current payroll taxes fund current benefits. Fifty years ago, over 40 workers paid in to Social Security for every one beneficiary. When Baby Boomers begin to retire, there will be fewer than three workers for every beneficiary.

It's not inconceivable that you could spend one-third or more of your life in retirement.

Given all these not-so-rosy facts, you would think Baby Boomers—76 million strong—would be pessimistic about retirement. On the contrary. In a 1998 survey by the American Association of Retired Persons (AARP), only about one-third said they expect to have to scale back their lifestyles during retirement. Maybe this optimistic attitude accounts for the fact that Boomers between the ages of 30 and 49 in 1996 had accumulated only about a third of what they're expected to need in retirement. To top off this Pollyanna attitude about future needs, the rate of personal savings has declined steadily over the past few decades and is now approaching historic lows.

So that's where we are when it comes to retirement. Overly optimistic. Pitifully prepared.

So what about you? Where do you stand individually when it

comes to retirement? Let's begin this look by assessing what you've stashed so far. Using the Future Value of Money chart from *The Complete Idiot's Guide® to Investing Like A Pro* on page 100, let's look at how much your current investment account should be worth on the day you retire. Here's what you do. Run your finger down the left-hand column until you get to the number of years you have left before retirement. Then move your finger across until you're under the percentage you're currently earning on your investment. The number you see here at the intersecting point is the value of one dollar at your retirement. Simply multiply the total dollars you have now by the number at the intersection of the rate of return percentage and year. For example, if you currently have $50,000 in your account earning 10-percent interest and have 20 years left before retirement, you would go down to 20 years and across to 10 percent. Then you would multiply $50,000 by 6.7275 (50,000 x 6.7275 = $336,375). So, when you retire, your $50,000 will have turned into $336,375.

Over periods of 20 years or more, the average return on a market-like portfolio has been around 10 to 12 percent. (The bull run starting in 1992 continuing through 1999 saw the S&P 500 averaging 19.18 percent annual gains.) To get a better sense of what to expect from different kinds of investments, here is a historical view of different categories and actual performance from Ibbotson Associates (as seen on www.Ibbotson.com).

COMPOUND ANNUAL RETURN 1926–1997

Standard & Poor's 500 Stock Index +11.0 percent

Long-Term Government Bonds Index +5.3 percent

U.S. Treasury Bills Index +3.8 percent

Inflation (Consumer Price Index) +3.1 percent

Source: Ibbotson Associates, 1998 Yearbook

THE FUTURE VALUE OF MONEY[5]
(Amount of $1 at Compound Interest)

Years	Rate 2%	4%	6%	8%	10%	12%
1	1.0200	1.0400	1.0600	1.0800	1.1000	1.1200
2	1.0404	1.0816	1.1236	1.1664	1.2100	1.2544
3	1.0612	1.1249	1.1910	1.2597	1.3310	1.4049
4	1.0824	1.1699	1.2625	1.3605	1.4641	1.5735
5	1.1041	1.2167	1.3382	1.4693	1.6105	1.7623
6	1.1262	1.2653	1.4185	1.5869	1.7716	1.9738
7	1.1487	1.3159	1.5036	1.7138	1.9487	2.2107
8	1.1717	1.3686	1.5938	1.8509	2.1436	2.4760
9	1.1951	1.4233	1.6895	1.9990	2.3579	2.7731
10	1.2190	1.4802	1.7908	2.1589	2.5937	3.1058
11	1.2434	1.5395	1.8983	2.3316	2.8531	3.4785
12	1.2682	1.6010	2.0122	2.5182	3.1384	3.8960
13	1.2936	1.6651	2.1329	2.7196	3.4523	4.3635
14	1.3195	1.7317	2.2609	2.9372	3.7975	4.8871
15	1.3459	1.8009	2.3965	3.1722	4.1772	5.4736
16	1.3728	1.8730	2.5403	3.4259	4.5950	6.1304
17	1.4002	1.9479	2.6928	3.7000	5.0545	6.8660
18	1.4282	2.0258	2.8543	3.9960	5.5599	7.6900
19	1.4568	2.1068	3.0256	4.3157	6.1159	8.6127
20	1.4859	2.1911	3.2071	4.6609	6.7275	9.6463
21	1.5157	2.2788	3.3995	5.0338	7.4002	10.8038
22	1.5460	2.3699	3.6035	5.4365	8.1403	12.1002
23	1.5769	2.4647	3.8197	5.8714	8.9543	113.5523
24	1.6084	2.5633	4.0489	6.3412	9.8497	15.1785
25	1.6406	2.6658	4.2918	6.8484	10.8346	16.9999
26	1.6734	2.7725	4.5494	7.3963	11.9181	19.0399
27	1.7069	2.8834	4.8223	7.9880	13.1099	21.3247
28	1.7410	2.9987	5.1117	8.6271	14.4209	23.8837
29	1.7758	3.1186	5.4184	9.3172	15.8630	26.7497
30	1.8113	3.2434	5.7435	10.0626	17.4493	29.9597
31	1.8476	3.3731	6.0881	10.8676	19.1942	33.5549
32	1.8845	3.5080	6.4533	11.7370	21.1136	37.5815
33	1.9222	3.6484	6.8405	12.6759	23.2250	42.0912
34	1.9607	3.7943	7.2510	13.6900	25.5475	47.1422
35	1.9999	3.9461	7.6860	14.7852	28.1022	52.7993
36	2.0399	4.1039	8.1472	15.9680	30.9125	59.1352
37	2.0807	4.2681	8.6360	17.2454	34.0037	66.2314
38	2.1223	4.4388	9.1542	18.6251	37.4041	74.1792
38	2.1647	4.6163	9.7034	20.1151	28.8157	83.0807
40	2.2080	4.8010	10.2856	21.7243	31.4092	93.0503

A NET-WORTH BALANCE SHEET VIEW
OF WHAT YOU HAVE

Knowing the future value of your current investments is important. Just as important, maybe more so, is having a measuring tool to assess what you have today and help measure your progress toward having more. That tool is the Net-Worth Balance Sheet.

Your net worth is figured by simply adding your assets and subtracting your debts and liabilities. The result is your net worth. There are scads of net-worth forms online and in bookstores. We've provided one here for your convenience. Simply copy the form and fill it out. Make this a habit once a year. Establish a date such as your anniversary date in Mary Kay or your birthday as the day you figure your net worth. Seeing that bottom line grow each year is a beautiful way to celebrate a special day.

When you're figuring your assets, place the values of your investments as they stand today. Figure the value of a car, your home and precious metals in the amount for which you could sell them for today. Your debt balances are the total amounts owed (not your minimum payments). If you follow the suggestions in this book by increasing your investments and savings while decreasing your debts, your net worth will continue to rise each year. Use your Net-Worth Statement as your yardstick for financial success.

STEP TWO: DETERMINE WHAT YOU'LL NEED

No one can predict the future—the inflation rate, interest rate or the cost of living in 20 to 30 years. So this exercise is a "best guess" based on advice from today's financial planners. We'll use a simple formula created by the American Savings Educational Council. The Ballpark Estimate Worksheet, reproduced in its entirety, assumes you will begin receiving Social Security at age 65, that you'll live to age 87, and you'll realize a constant real

NET-WORTH STATEMENT

Assets (what you have)

Investments

Retirement fund   _____

College fund   _____

Other mutual funds   _____

Stocks   _____

Bonds   _____

Rental property   _____

Accounts

Checking accounts   _____

Savings account   _____

CDs   _____

Money-market funds   _____

Stocks/bonds   _____

Treasury Bills   _____

Insurance cash values   _____

Home   _____

Cars   _____

Antiques, artwork, jewelry   _____

Personal property   _____

Other   _____

Total Assets (add all the above) $ _____

Liabilities (what you owe)

Mortgage(s)   _____

Car loans   _____

Student loans   _____

Bank loans   _____

Credit cards   _____

Other debt   _____

Total Liabilities (add all the above) $ _____

Net Worth (total assets minus
total liabilities) $ _____

rate of return of 3 percent after inflation. Whether this gets you to the exact dollar or not, going through this little exercise could pay off handsomely. According to the Employee Benefit Research Institute, people who had tried to figure out exactly what they would need for a comfortable retirement accumulated nearly five times as much as those who never tried to work it out. So here's your chance to open your eyes and boost the potential of your retirement fund.

THE BALLPARK ESTIMATE[6]

If you are married, you and your spouse should each fill out your own Ballpark Estimate worksheet taking your marital status into account when entering your Social Security benefit in number 2 below.

1. How much annual income will you want in retirement? (Figure 70% of your current annual household income just to maintain your current standard of living. Really.)   −$_____

2. Subtract the household income you expect to receive annually from:

  • Social Security, if you make under $25,000 enter $8,000; between $25,000 and $40,000, enter $12,000; over $40,000, enter $14,500 (for married couples—the lower earning spouse should enter either their own benefits based on their income or 50% of the higher earning spouse's benefit, whichever is higher)   −$_____

  • Traditional Employee Pension—a plan that pays a set dollar amount for life, where the dollar amount depends on salary and years of service (in today's dollars)   − $_____

  • Part-time income   − $_____

  • Other   − $_____

  **This is how much you need to make up
  for each retirement year**   = $_____

. . . The accountants went to work and devised this simple formula (so you could also know how much you'll need in the bank the day you retire to take care of this annual shortfall.)

3. To determine the amount you'll need to save, multiply
    the amount you need to make up by the factor below:

Age you expect to retire:	Your factor is:
55	21.0
60	18.9
65	16.4
70	13.6

    $_____

4. If you expect to retire before age 65, multiply your
    Social Security benefits from line 2 by the factor below:

Age you expect to retire:	Your factor is:
55	8.8
60	4.7

    + _____

5. Multiply your savings to date by the factor below
    (include money accumulated in your 401(K), IRA,
    or similar retirement plan):

If you want to retire in:	Your factor is:
10 years	1.3
15 years	1.6
20 years	1.8
25 years	2.1
30 years	2.4
35 years	2.8
40 years	3.3

    – $_____

    Total additional savings needed at retirement: = $_____

. . . Those same accountants devised another formula to show you how
much to save each year in order to reach your goal amount. They factored
in compounding. . . .

6. To determine the *annual* amount you'll need to save,
    multiply the *total* amount by the factor below:

If you want to retire: in:	Your factor is:
10 years	.085
15 years	.052
20 years	.036
25 years	.027
30 years	.020
35 years	.016
40 years	.013

    = $_____

This worksheet simplifies several planning issues such as projected Social
Security benefits and earnings assumptions on savings. It also reflects today's
dollars; therefore you will need to recalculate your retirement needs annually and as your salary and circumstances change. You may want to consider
doing further analysis, either by yourself using a more detailed worksheet or
computer software or with the assistance of a financial professional.

You may feel a real rate of return of 3 percent (that's the inflation percentage subtracted from the interest percentage you earn on your investment) is lower than what you think you will actually earn. If you're in a market portfolio, you may be right. If you would like to look at your figures using a different rate of return, go to the Invesco retirement calculator online. You'll be able to insert your rate of return and the program will do the calculations for you. Or speak to an Invesco* representative or other financial planner for a more detailed worksheet and different earnings assumptions on investments.

A few words about Social Security

If you've listened to the news, you've probably heard a variety of opinions about Social Security. As the program stands, it will begin to pay out more in benefits than it collects in payroll taxes soon after the Baby Boomers begin to retire. According to the National Commission on Retirement Policy, it will be entirely depleted by the year 2032. Various proposals are being considered regarding this program. The prudent course to take is twofold. First, be aware of the changes that will occur in this program in the next few years (they may involve tax considerations and work incentives). Second, understand that whatever changes are made to Social Security, ultimately in *today's* world, retirement security is a do-it-yourself kind of proposition.

If you want a more definitive look at Social Security and the benefits you can expect from the current program, you may call 1-800-772-1213 or visit the Social Security Web site at http://www.ssa.gov. After filling out the form SSA-7004, you will be sent your own Personal Earnings and Benefit Estimate Statement. It's a good idea to request a current statement every five years.

---

* Mary Kay Inc. does not endorse Invesco or in any way warrant, represent or guarantee the safety or the rate of return of any investment with Invesco.

STEP THREE:
CREATE AN ACTION PLAN TO GET YOU THERE

The do-it-yourself options

Individual Retirement Accounts. When it became clear that Social Security was going to start running out of money in the 21st century, the government introduced Individual Retirement Accounts in the early 1980s. The idea was to give everyone a convenient way to save for retirement. The IRA rules allow you to contribute $2,000 a year until April 15 and count it as a deduction for the previous year (if you qualify). You may fully deduct your contribution if your gross income is not more than $35,000 if single or $50,000 if you're married and filing jointly.

Keogh plans. The Keogh plan was named for the U.S. Representative who introduced it in the 1960s. Keoghs are for self-employed individuals and are flexible when it comes to contributions. You can contribute a fixed percentage of your income (up to $30,000) or a variable portion of your earnings or nothing at all. But whatever you choose, you must stick to it. If you contribute a fixed percentage of income one year, then you can't switch to a variable portion the next.

401(k) plans. This plan is for people who are employed by companies with 25 or more employees. It allows employees to contribute a combination of taxable and pretax dollars into an account that offers a variety of investments (typically mutual funds that invest in stocks, bonds and money markets). By the way, the plan's "401" designation refers to the paragraph number in the Internal Revenue Code where this plan is described.

Simplified Employee Pension (SEP) plans. This plan is for the self-employed like you and me and acts much like an IRA or Keogh plan. Using some SEP plans, you may contribute 1 percent to 10 percent of your compensation (excluding compensation in excess of $160,000) to your account in any given year. Your dollars grow without being taxed, which means you have more dollars growing and more interest compounding. Remember the magic of compounding? Well, having a tax-deferred investment has a little magic in it too. For example, if you placed $2,000 a year earning 7 percent in a taxable account for 25 years, your result would be $91,078.61. In a tax-deferred account, the result would be $126,498.08—over $35,000 difference! The combination of tax-deferring and compounding works wonders for a retirement account. Of course, you pay taxes on the money when you take it out after you're 59-½, but more than likely you'll find yourself in a lower tax bracket after you retire, so the tax-bite won't be as great.

And here's another tax consideration that makes a SEP account such a smart decision. You can deduct your SEP contribution up to 13.04 percent of your net earnings from your income tax. Let's run this through with actual numbers so you get the full impact of this little tax perk. Let's say that after you deduct business expenses, home office deduction and self-employment tax, your net earnings are $25,000 and your federal income tax rate is 28 percent. Your federal income tax will be $25,000 X .28 = $7,000.

Now, let's say you decide to invest 13.04 percent of your $25,000 net earnings in your SEP-IRA account. This 13.04 percent of $25,000 would be $3,260. Of course, this investment is deductible so off that $25,000 you take $3,260 more ($25,000 – $3,260 = $21,740. Guess what! You just dropped from the 28-percent to the 15-percent tax bracket which means the amount of federal income tax you owe dropped too from $7,000 to $3,261 ($21,740 X .15 = $3,261). You just saved $3,739 on your tax bill and tucked away over $3,000 for your future. Smart!

LESSON IN STARTING EARLY AND STAYING THE COURSE

When I was a new Mary Kay Independent Sales Director in New England, I held a skin-care class one evening at the nurses' dormitory of a local Boston hospital. My hostess had a guest departing just as I was arriving, a young man she said was preparing her taxes. I laughed and commented that I would be needing such a service since I was self-employed and had a "new position" in leadership which would greatly increase my income. Obviously, I would need good tax records.

We exchanged business cards and immediately connected. He was very thorough and followed up with my request. Not only did he prepare my taxes, he followed the tax discussion by saying, "Now we have to talk about setting you up with a tax-deferred savings plan. It will involve a small monthly contribution and the account will grow steadily if you leave it alone. It will make a nice retirement fund for you and your family." I laughed, thinking it to be a bit premature. I had three children under the age of 6 at the time and no thought or plan for the fourth that ultimately arrived!

Although I had laughed, I could tell he was serious, so I yielded to a small monthly plan of contributing $25 a month. It seems so insignificant when I think about it now. But with monitoring, his on-going advice, and increasing contributions as my business grew, that small beginning is not so small anymore.

Thank goodness he had the right idea of being more to me than a tax accountant and thank goodness I had the presence of mind to comply and to get on board! Today he is a partner in one of the most successful accounting firms in Boston and I am an Independent National Sales Director with Mary Kay! My willingness to cooperate and to never touch the accounts (even though I was tempted many times along the way when funds were tight) has allowed me to look at all those dizzying zeroes with tremendous pride! That million-dollar account is a reality!

— ANNE NEWBURY, Independent Executive National Sales Director

The Mary Kay Family Security Plan for Independent National Sales Directors. Of course, you have one more option when planning for your future—a plan specific to Mary Kay and reserved for the elite of the elite—Independent National Sales Directors. This plan is called the Family Security Program and provides protection for NSDs and their families through life insurance, plus valuable retirement and disability benefits.

A final thought about retiring a millionaire. If you think about the wealthiest people in this country, it's rare to find any who are employed by someone else. Think about it. Bill Gates, Warren Buffett, Donald Trump, Ross Perot, Steven Spielberg—the truly wealthy are typically truly *free* to create and build and grow as large and as wonderful as they'd like. You have that option with Mary Kay. The status of Independent National Sales Director with Mary Kay has millionaire written all over her! Start now with your SEP account, contribute consistently to it and aim toward that million-dollar target on your calendar. But if you want a boost, also aim for National Sales Director status and give your million-dollar goal two times the power.

Fact: Federal Estate Tax Return Form 706 must generally be filed and taxes paid by the estate within nine months following the estate owner's death.

LESSON IN RETIRING A MILLIONAIRE

*M*y husband and I planned a million-dollar retirement together. Our goal also is to live debt-free as part of the plan. We regularly give to the Lord (at least 10 percent of our income), save and invest in growth opportunities in mutual funds (primarily in global technology and blue-chip stocks). I've set up a separate retirement account that's tax-deferred and a college education fund for each of our three children, providing them $100,000 each by the time they are 18 years old. I make regular contributions from my Mary Kay income every month through an automatic deposit, dedicated and used for the above-outlined allocations. Our goal as a couple is not just financial. We want to empower and enrich the lives of other couples. Our long-term plan includes leaving a legacy of knowledge, and encouraging and mentoring other couples toward healthy, successful relationships as spouses, parents and leaders in their respective business communities. That's the real beauty of a million-dollar retirement. It will allow us to realize our purpose of helping other couples. We can do that with financial security. A million-dollar goal gives us more choices.

— **LISE CLARK**, Independent Executive Senior Sales Director

Goal #4: A life that realizes your purpose

This goal takes a lifetime to achieve. This goal may not be *directly* financial; however, money does play a part in helping you achieve it. It's simple really—if you have the money you need to cover the basics, you'll have the security to think beyond survival. When you tick off "food and shelter" on the bottom rung of Maslow's Hierarchy of Needs (a theory explaining people's motivation), you're able to step up the chart all the way to the top rung of human needs—the need for self-actualization. By fulfilling this need, you're becoming the best you can be, you are realizing Mary Kay's dream for you, you are living your values, you are doing what you came here to do.

For example, I believe I came here to raise two wonderful, independent, self-confident, principle-centered young men (my two sons). I also came here to communicate to as many people as possible the joys of living with honor, integrity, humanity, charity of spirit and spiritual peace. This is taking me a lifetime to accomplish.

It may be now that you're doing what you came here to do, or it may be later. Some people need the luxury of time supplied by retirement to realize their vision. That's OK! Mary Kay started Mary Kay Cosmetics after she retired from her first career. Keep your vision clearly before you and if it is to be realized after retirement, even more reason to create a million-dollar plan.

Stepping back and taking this long-term view is great for getting the full picture, but remember, it's the *living* day to day with consistency of purpose that will get you to the achievement of this goal. Commit to it, live it, achieve it!

Goal #5: A legacy of peace and prosperity for your heirs

When we talk of leaving a legacy, we're broadening the definition of legacy beyond that usually given by an attorney or financial planner. A legacy is more than a gift of property. A legacy is a gift of love, of wisdom, of spirit. This kind of legacy takes moment-by-moment living from the heart. Some financial experts recognize the importance of this kind of legacy and even go so far as to say that the only road to success is one of service, of doing for others, of living what we know as a "Go-Give" kind of existence. If you listen carefully to the talks of our most successful Independent Sales Directors and National Sales Directors, you will hear in their "how-to" explanations a common theme—help others get what they want and you will get what you want. Service. Giving for the benefit of others. Living from your heart and leaving behind the warmth of it with everyone you touch. That's the legacy Mary Kay Ash has left us, and the one that describes the legacy you may leave others. We'll talk more about the benefits—both financial and spiritual—of giving in Chapter 8.

For now, let's talk about the other side of "legacy"—the property side. Maybe you've thought that estate planning was something for the wealthy and not a topic of real concern for you. So let's begin by clearing up a few common misconceptions.

1. Some people think if they don't have a large estate, they don't really need a will. If you or your husband dies intestate (without a will), *any* assets you own without beneficiary designations will be divided by a judge in probate court according to the laws of your state. You may not be too concerned about this since the house, cars and bank accounts will likely pass to the spouse and children due to beneficiary designations, which are exactly your wishes anyway. A will, however, has other functions which will have a significant impact on the legacy you leave. One is the will's function of guardian designation for your children. Without a will, a judge will decide who raises your children and manages the money you've set aside for them. You're in the best position to make that decision, so keep that decision in your hands with a will. No matter what the size of your estate, if you're a parent of minor children, you need a will.

2. Your estate is not simply the land and home in which you live. Your estate is all of your possessions—even your life insurance proceeds plus all taxable investments such as stocks, bonds, money markets, all IRAs and employer-sponsored retirement plan benefits, your home equity, business interests, cars, boats, jewelry, furniture, collectibles, clothing—*everything.*

3. Estate taxes are *not* on the same scale as income tax. Estate taxes (the tax assessed to your heirs after you die) start at 37 percent and run as high as 55 percent. You may have a million dollars' worth of assets to leave your kids, but without smart estate planning, the government could take half of it before it gets to them. And remember, *all* your assets add up to create your estate and resulting estate tax bill. That may mean your children would have to sell the less-liquid assets, such as your home and belongings, in order to get the cash to pay the government. Since estate taxes are due within nine months following the estate owner's death, this puts a "fire-sale" mentality into play which isn't the best atmosphere for getting what your property is worth.

General rule of thumb about life insurance: Generally buy life insurance in the amount of five times your annual salary.

4. Maybe you're still not concerned about estate taxes because you've heard about the unified credit that virtually makes you exempt from estate taxes on an estate under $675,000, so you don't feel you're affected. Let's take a long-term look at this idea. Yes, you do receive an exemption from paying taxes on an estate that does not exceed $675,000 in the year 2000. And the good news is that this unified credit amount goes up to $1,000,000 for each individual by the year 2006. But here's the thing to consider: the value of your estate is going to go up too. You may not have assets that add up to over a million dollars now, but what about in the year 2010 or 2020? Remember the future value of a dollar chart on page 100? Estimate the value of your estate right now. Use the chart to calculate the value of these total dollars in 30 to 40 years. Is that amount over the $1,000,000 mark? Do you need to think about estate planning now?

TAX-SAVING OPTIONS

Getting your estate organized in order to save income taxes now and save estate taxes later is a complicated process with a variety of options. The best idea is to read this section and get familiar with the high points, and then go to a tax attorney or estate planner to pursue specific options. Individual state laws differ and federal laws typically change. The message here is, simply, don't put off estate planning. Here are a few possible tax-saving options:

- There is one big deduction you can take on your estate—the unlimited marital deduction. Here's the gist—you can deduct from your estate the value of all assets you pass on to your spouse either by a will or in a trust. Now you're thinking, hey, you scare me with that 55-percent tax bite thing and then tell me my taxes are zip if I leave my estate to my spouse. So what's the problem? Here it is . . . your spouse doesn't have that option anymore—you're no longer around so there's no marital deduction he can take. When he passes away, there is that pesky estate tax again just as menacing as before. And to make it worse, the unified credit exclusion is based on an individual's maximum amount at that point. The same estate now has half of the tax exclusion credit.

    The professionals give this alternative to passing on the entire estate directly to your spouse. A smarter option is to divide your assets in half and will only half to your spouse and use the other half to set up a credit shelter trust. Your spouse gets all the income generated by the trust's investments while he's alive and then the principal is passed on to your children when your husband dies. These are just the high points of this strategy. Get the details from a tax attorney or estate planner.

• Another option is to set up a charitable trust that allows you to pass your assets to a charity at your death, but allows the income generated by the trust to go to the surviving spouse while that spouse is alive. You get a charitable gift deduction on your income taxes while you're alive, and the assets in the trust are excluded from your estate when estate taxes are being figured. You may be thinking you would prefer your assets to go to your children. You can have the best of both worlds by using an Irrevocable Life Insurance Trust or Wealth Replacement Trust that would essentially give your children the same value of your estate when you die (no taxes are due on life insurance benefits).

Here is how it works according to Tim C. Fitzgerald, Accredited Estate Planner: "You can use some of the Charitable Remainder Trust income to make gifts to an Irrevocable Life Insurance Trust (ILIT). This trust can provide life insurance for your heirs to help replace the assets going to charity at your death. The gifts may reduce your net estate, thereby reducing estate taxes. Your heirs receive your net estate after estate taxes and expenses, plus life insurance proceeds from the ILIT."

Again, there are variations to this strategy. The point—take this knowledge to a professional and take your estate planning forward from there.

• Here's another nifty option for reducing estate taxes. Start giving to your children while you're alive. You're allowed to give $10,000 per person per year ($20,000 if you're making a joint gift with your husband) in order to reduce your estate and as a result reduce your estate tax.

Again, this is simply a top-line look at estate-planning issues. The message here is to think about your goal of leaving a legacy and start planning for the fulfillment of that goal right now. Living from your heart will assure your children the emotional and spiritual gifts they deserve. Living from your head will assure them the physical gifts they deserve. Do both and leave the legacy befitting the woman you are.

Use today's bonuses for tomorrow's goals

We've talked a lot about setting aside dollars to make extra payments on your mortgage, setting aside dollars to build a college fund for your children, setting aside dollars to build your million-dollar retirement. Wow—that's a lot of dollars! You may be dragging right now thinking you barely make the utility bill payments, much less scare up an extra hundred here and hundred there for long-term goals. The solution is in your own backyard. Use your business to secure your future. For instance, if you are an Independent Sales Director, make those "extra" mortgage payments and college and retirement fund contributions by using the bonus plan that's in front of you. Let's start by taking a look at the difference building offspring Sales Directors could make to your long-term goals. Take a look at the difference one year of building could make:

Living from your heart will assure your children
the emotional and spiritual gifts they deserve.
Living from your head will assure them the physical
gifts they deserve.

OFFSPRING OPPORTUNITIES

How profitable can building offspring Independent Sales Directors be?

	ONE OFFSPRING SALES DIRECTOR	FOUR OFFSPRING SALES DIRECTORS	SEVEN OFFSPRING SALES DIRECTORS
Tier 1*			
(production $4,000–$11,999)			
Wholesale production	$9,000	$36,000	$63,000
Commission	x 4%	x 4.5%	x 5%
Monthly income	360	1,620	3,150
Months	x 12	x 12	x 12
Annual income from Offspring Sales Directors	**$4,320**	**$19,440**	**$37,800**
Tier 2*			
(production $12,000 or more)			
Wholesale production	$9,000	$36,000	$63,000
Commission	x 5%	x 5.5%	x 6%
Monthly income	450	1,980	3,780
Months	x 12	x 12	x 12
Annual income from offspring Sales Directors	**$5,400**	**$23,760**	**$45,360**

Building People= Building Income

Shown are just a few examples** of the annual earning potential offspring Sales Directors can provide.

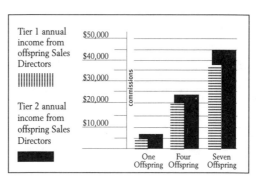

* Senior and Executive Senior Sales Directors are paid at the Tier 2 commission rate when their personal unit monthly wholesale production is $12,000 or more and also for three months after the debut of a new offspring Sales Director.

**The example shown in the chart and graph above assumes that each offspring Sales Director achieves $9,000 monthly unit wholesale production.

What could you do with an extra $37,800 this year? Why leave this money on the table? Wouldn't you prefer it growing in your retirement account or securing equity in your home?

And here's another source of "extra" cash just waiting for you to claim it—the Unit Development Bonus.

3 new qualified* unit members in month 1	$ 300
3 new qualified unit members in month 2	$ 300
3 new qualified unit members in month 3	$ 300
Total monthly bonuses	$ 900
9 or more for calendar quarter	+$ 600
Total bonuses for calendar quarter	$1,500

* A qualified team member is one whose initial order with the Company is $600 or more in wholesale Section 1 products and it is received and accepted by the Company in the same or following calendar month her Independent Beauty Consultant Agreement is received and accepted by the Company.

The $300 Sales Director Unit Development Bonus is earned in the month in which the qualified team members' initial minimum $600 wholesale Section 1 orders (at least three) are received and accepted by the Company. The $600 Sales Director Unit Development Bonus is earned in the calendar quarter in which the qualified team members' initial minimum $600 wholesale Section 1 orders (at least nine) are received and accepted by the Company. A calendar quarter is either: 1) January, February and March; 2) April, May and June; 3) July, August and September; or 4) October, November and December. Sales Director Commission and Sales Director Bonuses will be paid on the basis of wholesale orders and Agreement received and accepted by the Company by the end of the business day the last working day of the month.

There, sitting on the table, is an extra $1,500 a quarter if you choose to maximize this plan. That's $6,000 a year of "above-and-beyond" money to apply to your goals. Think about this one bonus alone and the value of compounding over the next 20 years. If you maximize the plan just one year—this year—and set aside that $6,000 in an investment account earning 12 percent interest, that $6,000 will turn into $57,877.80 when you need it for retirement 20 years from now.

Take advantage of all these bonus and commission dollars, invest them consistently and watch out! Millionaire destiny could be *your* destiny!

Six Most Important Things to Do to Take the Long-Term Look

1. Find out the principal portion of your monthly mortgage payment and start paying that extra principal a month to your mortgage company or setting it aside in your retirement account.

2. Project college costs for your children using the chart on page 93. Then start building toward this projection.

3. Assess the future value of the savings/investment accounts you currently have using the chart on page 100. Use the Ballpark Estimate on page 103–104 to determine what you'll need to make up from there for a comfortable retirement.

4. Open your SEP-IRA account and start making up the difference.

5. Calculate the value of your estate in 30 to 40 years using the Future Value of Money chart on page 100.

6. Maximize the dollars available to you as an Independent Sales Director (for unit development and offspring Sales Directors). Apply this "extra" money to your long-term goals.

Definitions of Living Rich

Making and living the choices in your life.
—*Julie Hattabaugh*

Helping other women to achieve excellence.
—*Ann Geier*

Having the opportunity to keep my integrity and to develop
and empower my personal character. I can be me!
—*Ina O'Neil*

Being able to do what I want, when I want and
with whom I want to do it.
—*Karen Bonura*

Having healthy, wonderful, positive, confident children.
—*Valerie Spencer*

Waking up excited and positive every day.
—*Beth Morales*

Working with my daughter in Mary Kay.
—*Deanna Spillman*

Having the time to do what I want to do when I want to do it.
—*Sandra Braun*

Being able to choose anything—whether it's education for my
children or a fantasy vacation—but always having choices
and opportunity.
—*Wendy Hayum-Gross*

Living a Rich Life

CHAPTER SIX

Law #6: Join the BIDIA Club

You are thinking the same thoughts those who achieved greatness did, facing the same obstacles they faced. They too had small children, they worked full-time jobs, had teenagers, were single parents, had PMS and menopause and depression and vacations and holidays and lazy days and they even had bad-hair days. But they became members of something we call the "BIDIA" club—"But I Did It Anyway"—whatever it took. — MARY KAY ASH

LET'S GET REALLY PRACTICAL HERE—everyday folding-the-under-wear kind of practical. After all, living a rich life isn't always glamorous. For instance, digging the dirt from underneath your kid's fingernails isn't glamorous, but you have to do it anyway if you want a healthy kid and appreciative looks from the teacher on PTA nights—a couple of living-rich sort of things. Now it's time we talk about other living-rich sort of things that take the same "but I did it anyway" kind of discipline. In other words, it's time to gut up and get ready to deal with the kind of issues that need to get done because the better you do them, the richer you'll be. Simple topics—rich results.

*If you prepare an income statement
once a month, you'll be able to get a grip
on the ins and outs of your money.*

Budgeting, for instance. We'll start there. Then we'll move into ways to spend less followed by things to consider when buying a home, building an emergency fund and choosing the right insurance plans. Now stay with me here. Remember, Mary Kay's formula for success has always been about self-reliance, self-discipline and self-control. Obviously, from Mary Kay's perspective, a *man* is not a *plan*. *You* are the plan when it comes to success . . . when it comes to living rich. This is your chapter to help devise that plan. Get out your journal; you may want to make some new commitments!

BIDIA budgeting

Let's just jump right into this one. Remember in Chapter 2 the two types of people defined by Henry Brock—the type who spends first and saves what's left and the type who saves first and spends what's left? Only one in 20 saves first and spends what's left—more than likely the same one in 20 who lives with a budget. A budget is not a record of what happened with your money; it's a plan of what *should* happen. Approach it this way. Take the percentage you plan to give to your church or charity and the percentage you plan to save right off the top—write the checks, put them in the envelopes, address the envelopes, stamp them and send them on their way. Then look at what you have left over. You may need to reallocate the remaining dollars according to your spending priorities. I didn't say this would be easy. You need to sit down with your husband and decide if you're going to change to a give-and-save-first, spend-later kind of budget or if you're going to stay as you are—either recording past spending habits and pretending you have a budget or ignoring the whole thing. If you're the one in 20 who is taking the savings off the top, congratulations! You have this BIDIA budgeting down cold. If you haven't quite mastered it, here are some suggestions based on the advice of financial consultant Henry S. Brock[1] to help you create a spending plan and stick to it:

1. maintain respectful communication with your husband;
2. place your "future" dollars on top—the dollars you save or invest;
3. accept full responsibility for your decisions;
4. avoid impulse spending—the "gotta have it now" disease;
5. view your budget as liberating rather than restrictive (a budget frees the dollars that will ultimately help you realize your goals).

*It's best to avoid taking a loan
to finance assets that lose value over time,
such as furniture, clothing and cars.*

You've probably seen all kinds of examples of budget worksheets. They're everywhere. Of all the ones I found, here is my favorite, created by CNBC business journalist Bill Griffeth:[2]

MONTHLY BUDGET

Category	Budget	Actual	Actual
Prosperity Dollars			
My 401(k)			
Our reserve account			
College account #1			
College account #2			
Budget Dollars			
Mortgage			
Phone			
Electricity/water			
Gas			
Auto fuel			
Cable TV			
Our cash allowance			
Our checking account			
Our date			
Deficit Dollars			
Auto loan #1			
Auto loan #2			
Credit card #1			
Credit card #2			

As you see, the dollars to secure your future are placed right on top. Top priority. Add your giving dollars up there too and you'll have a give-and-save-first model to live by. Then success will be built right into this budget. Notice deficit dollars are last. These are the ones you should try to erase completely from your outgo (more about how in Chapter 9).

You may want to copy this page and use it for your budgeting, or here's a suggestion. Get a personal finance software package for your computer. If a computer can morph hairstyles atop your head as you stand before a kiosk in the mall, just think what it could do for your budget. You'll also find budget worksheets online. Just use a search engine and type in "budget worksheet" and watch all the choices that appear before you. Take your pick and fill it out according to what you think you're spending in each category. As you see, savings is a category on the budget right along with utilities and mortgage payments. Fill in the blank in the amount you determined earlier you need to commit to college funds and retirement. You'll also need an emergency fund, so set aside a few dollars to build that as well (more about emergency funds on page 139).

WHO PAYS AND HOW MUCH?

Now you have your budget. You see the plan for spending and the dollars needed to cover the expenses. The next challenge is to divvy up the dollars from your income to cover these expenses. If you're married and your family income comes from your work as well as your husband's, the question to answer next is, who pays and how much?

Here's one answer suggested by a variety of experts: Divide up expenses based on your percentage of income in relationship to the whole. For example, let's take a hypothetical. Household expenses for our example (including investments) total around $4,200 a month. One spouse brings in a net income of $3,500 a month. The other spouse earns a net income of $2,000 a month, making the total household net income $5,500 a month. To divide the expenses in half (each spouse paying $2,100 a month toward expenses) obviously wouldn't be the fair distribution of responsibility. A better idea is to divide payment responsibility on the same percentage as the income contribution. The spouse earning $3,500 a month contributes 64 percent to the income ($3,500 divided by $5,500) and the spouse earning $2,000 contributes 36 percent ($2,000 divided by $5,500). So the 64 percenter should pay 64 percent of the expenses ($2,688) and the 36 percenter should pay 36 percent of the expenses ($1,512). The combined discretionary dollars of $812 and $488 could go into the household account, creating $1,300 each month to cover unexpected expenses or build toward future purchases. Or this combined $1,300 in discretionary income could be divided between partners and become exactly that—discretionary—left in individual accounts (yours and your husband's) to spend however each of you like. If you're out of debt and have taken your necessary savings and investments off the top and still have this discretionary money left over, have a ball!

NOW TAKE AN ACTUAL SNAPSHOT OF SPENDING HABITS

If what you see after filling out your first budget sheet is the proverbial "more month than money" problem, you need to make a change. The experts recommend the first thing you do is find the holes—the leaks where dollars are dribbling out of your hands every month. That takes discipline. You have to take a deep breath and focus on every penny you spend—not forever, just long enough to capture on paper the real ins and outs of your money (experts recommend around three months). Make it easy on yourself—pick up a little notebook and pen that slips easily into your purse. Then when you stop by the cash machine, write down the amount you pocket. When you charge dinner after a soccer game on your charge card, write it down. Then at the end of the month, look at your checkbook and record the checks you wrote under the appropriate categories on your budget worksheet. Record the spending decisions on your budget as listed in your diary. After three months of recording your actual spending decisions, you'll begin to see the patterns. Too much cash slipping through a black hole after leaving the Automatic Teller Machine? Too many impulse buys slapped on your American Express® or Visa®? Writing more checks for your children's sports than you realized? That interest on your MasterCard® eating you alive? You're kissing off money right and left! Not a pretty sight, but at least you now see it and have a better chance of plugging up the holes.

BIDIA CHANGES TO SPENDING DECISIONS

Throwing money at all those things on a "want" list is a natural response for most people. It just feels good, right? Well, if you want to move into the black on your budget, it may be time to make a shift in your thinking. Three concepts suggested by the money experts really made me view spending differently. Maybe they'll have the same impact on you.

1. The first one involves peeling off the pretty paper from a purchase and looking at it in terms of how much it really cost you. Because of sales tax and income tax, what you actually pay for an item is much more than what's on the price tag. Generally speaking, it takes $2 in gross earnings for every $1 you spend. Because consumption is the most heavily taxed activity you could possibly do, it's also the most expensive thing you could possibly do.

2. The next brain shift involves a "swap" mentality as you view a purchase. Typically our eyes are focused solely on that pretty new thing we're buying. We write that check as fast as we can or race through the signature on that charge slip so we can get that pretty little thing in our hands and out the door. But wait a minute. In your hands prior to the purchase, you had economic power—power that store owner desperately wants. You just "swapped" that power

for that thing. If you think this way, when you stand at the checkout counter, your focus will be on both the pretty little new thing in the sales clerk's hands *and* the economic power in yours. Now your thinking will not be that you're making a purchase, rather you're making a "swap." Sounds simple, but next time you read the pricetag on something you "want," think of those dollars as economic power. Do you really want to swap that power for that item?

"Wealth is largely a result of habit."

JOHN JACOB ASTOR

3. And to add even more fuel to your spending discipline, here's one more brain twist to apply to spending. Not only should you think of a purchase price in terms of the double amount you have to earn to account for the heavy taxation of consumption, not only should you think in terms of swapping economic power for that expenditure, you should also add this little nugget to your thinking. Look at those dollars you're giving up in terms of lost-opportunity cost. What would those dollars mean in the future if you didn't spend them now? The lost-opportunity cost of $100 spent now is actually $965 twenty years from now if it had been invested in an account with a 12-percent return rather than being spent. The lost-opportunity cost then of that $100 jacket is actually $965. Is the jacket worth it? It is if you need a jacket to keep you warm. Then the jacket becomes a "need." It may *not* be if the warmth issue is covered and this jacket is strictly in the "gotta-be-me, gotta-be-cool" category. You decide. But if you need the discipline to scale down expenses, make your decisions using these new ways to think about consumption as a part of your internal discussion.

LESSON IN SPENDING AND SELF-CONFIDENCE

When I started my Mary Kay business, I was afraid of money. I was afraid to talk about it because I had been raised in a family in which it was considered in poor taste to discuss anything concerning money. I was afraid to make a lot of money, afraid to take charge of money, and afraid to know where it was going. The one thing I was not afraid to do was to spend it! I spent wildly with no plan or thought of the consequences. I buried my head in the sand, did not balance my checkbook or take personal responsibility for credit-card balances. However, as my income grew, so did my self-confidence. As I began to realize what a competent and capable person I was, I began to turn toward my money in an embracing way. I began to make conscious choices of how to spend and save it. As my spiritual relationship with God grew, I also began to see the sin of squandering and excess. That became a driving force and over the last three years I have paid off all my debt, reduced spending to what is necessary and have become passionately excited about saving. I have reduced my wardrobe to essential pieces that work together and do not buy clothes impulsively. As a result, I feel so much more authentic in my representation of this tremendous opportunity and very capable of leading other women to financial freedom and success. **—JACKIE ROOT, Independent Senior Sales Director**

Now that you have the discipline down pat, you may be up for the challenge of putting that discipline to the test. Here are a few opportunities:

Ways to spend less

- Wait two weeks for major purchases.
- Keep a journal of all your purchases.
- Wait until you have the money before you buy something.
- Take care of what you have. Regular oil changes on your car extend the life of the engine. Dusting the coils on your

refrigerator saves energy and could save your refrigerator. Cleaning or replacing your air conditioner filters cuts energy costs. Using a soaker hose around your home helps protect your foundation.

- Wear it out. Think about how much you could save if you decided to use items 20 percent longer.

- Do it yourself. Whenever you're thinking of calling in an expert for a fix-it job, ask yourself, "Can I do this myself? What would it take to learn how?" When the gray hair creeps into your reflection in the mirror, could you color it yourself? When you need a manicure . . . you get the idea.

- Comparison-shop by phone or online.

- Substitute a generic brand for the name brand.

- Shampoo your pooch in your shower instead of at the doggie salon. Think of the bonding opportunity!

- Never buy on impulse. Walk away and think.

- Use coupons when you grocery shop and don't go down those aisles hungry!

- Vacation during off-season. Rates are typically less.

- Eat at home more often.

- Avoid carrying a balance on your credit cards. Use credit cards carefully.

- Make extra principal payments on your home and pay off your mortgage earlier.

- Take your investment contributions right off the top of your income. Pay everyone else next.

- Raise the deductible on your insurance. By taking your deductible from $100 or $250 to $500 or $1,000, you may be able to cut your premiums by 10 percent to 20 percent or more. And what if you have a claim? That's why you have an emergency fund. (Use the savings on premiums to help build your emergency fund.)

- When you buy a car, check the Internet for lowest prices. Shop around for financing—don't just accept the dealer's rate. Owning a car for at least eight years maximizes your investment.

- Better yet, earn the use of a Mary Kay career car. Why make a car payment when you can drive virtually for free? Take the $350 or $400 you would have paid for a car each month and stick it into an investment account. Investing $350 a month at 12-percent return for 25 years will create for you $657,596.32. Talk about opportunity!

BIDIA habits

Sometimes staying on budget-alert gets tough. That's when you simply have to get tougher. Here is a review of the habits that will help you do so:

- Make yourself an invoice for savings and stack it on top of your bills.

- Determine your real spendable income (after you've deducted your giving choices, savings, investment contributions and mortgage prepayment obligations).

- Establish spending limits.

- Categorize your expenses.

- At the end of each month write down the amounts you spent in each category.

- Keep a handy journal and write down all your expenditures when they happen.

- If you happen upon something you want that costs more than your spendable limit, put it back and wait.

LESSON IN TAKING PERSONAL RESPONSIBILITY

When I was growing up, we were rich in faith in God and a work ethic, but we lacked resources and opportunities. We lived in a small four-room house that my dad built. We cooked our food on a cookstove fired by wood and heated the house with a coal-fueled black pot-bellied stove. We didn't have indoor plumbing until I was 5. I can remember picking strawberries for a nickel a quart and bunching daffodils to send to the city to be sold. I cleaned, ironed and did anything I could to make money. I had my first "business" when I was 10. I sold Fashion Frock dresses door-to-door. When I was 15, I got a job as a carhop at a drive-in across from my high school. I married Kirk when I was 17. We had three children by the time I was 23. When I stumbled upon a Mary Kay career, I had intended to make $30 a week for extras. Amazing things happened. Everything Mary Kay said, I took to heart and put into practice. I started making very good money! That's when I adopted the attitude that there was an unending supply of money out there and I spent accordingly. My husband took the job of "managing the money." I thought things were going great. The income kept increasing. I became an Independent National Sales Director. Because Kirk didn't want to demotivate me, he robbed Peter to pay Paul believing that surely I would come to my senses eventually and get in charge of my spending. Finally, Kirk decided that it was time I took full responsibility. He "resigned" his position as money manager of the family and "gave" it all to me. It was a stressful time because I knew nothing about computers and little about accounting and money management, but I learned. I now do an automatic withdrawal from my commission checks into an Invesco* money market to save for quarterly taxes. I have learned to know what I'm paying for, to negotiate the best rates, to trim unnecessary expenses and plan for future expenditures. Every woman needs to know how to manage money and save for the future. Of course, you can't "manage" money if you have no control over spending. This has been a painful but valuable lesson for us. I'll never forget the day Kirk said to me, "Sue, even a millionaire will go broke when she's spending a million and a half." It was a wake-up call for me to take personal responsibility for being a good steward with what we have been entrusted. If someone else can learn from this lesson, then I consider the experience even more valuable.

—SUE KIRKPATRICK, Independent National Sales Director

---

* Mary Kay Inc. does not endorse Invesco or in any way warrant, represent or guarantee the safety or the rate of return of any investment with Invesco.

BIDIA HOME BUYING

Buying a home is a huge undertaking, but most of the time, it makes economic good sense, so here is another one of those "but I did it anyway" kinds of financial decisions. The cash needed to close the average American home is around $28,000. That's a lot, of course, but you can do it if you decide you will, if you arm yourself with the information you need to establish meaningful goals and if you follow a savings plan to get you there.

Let's take a closer look at that average home requiring cash in the amount of $28,000. If you save $500 a month getting a 12-percent return, you should have the cash you need in about four years. It can be done. Naturally, the amount of cash you need specifically will depend on the cost of the house you plan to buy. And *that* will depend on what you can afford the cost of the house to be.

To figure that bit of information, let's use the same factors a lender uses when deciding if a home loan will be approved or denied. Lenders look at two things:

1. Your loan-to-value percentage
2. Your long-term debt percentage

Loan-to-value percentage

The first factor, the loan-to-value percentage, is determined by the size of the downpayment you're planning to make. If the loan you're applying for is $90,000 and the value of the property is $100,000, then the loan-to-value percentage is 90 percent. Your downpayment takes care of the other 10 percent. Typically, lenders use your loan-to-value percentage to determine the maximum monthly mortgage payment you can afford to make. For instance, if your loan-to-value percentage is 90 percent, a lender will allow your monthly mortgage payment (that's principal and interest) to be up to 25 percent of your gross monthly income. If your loan-to-value percentage is 80 percent (you're making a

20 percent downpayment), then lenders allow your mortgage payment to be up to 38 percent of your gross monthly income.

Here's an example of each size of downpayment. First, the 10 percent downpayment: If your loan-to-value percentage is 90 percent and your gross monthly income is $5,000, your lender will multiply $5,000 by .25 to determine the maximum monthly payment you can afford to make. Using these numbers, that maximum is $1,250.

Let's say you increased your downpayment to 20 percent, making your loan-to-value percentage 80 percent. Now your lender will multiply $5,000 by .38, which is $1,900. Remember, this is a total monthly payment that includes principal, interest, taxes and insurance. Also keep this in mind: Your lender may allow up to 38 percent of your gross income to be applied to your mortgage payment, but you may have other plans. For instance, if you have a shorter time-frame than 30 years until your mortgage-burning date, you definitely want to use a lower percentage so you can escalate your payments to meet that goal. Also, you may want to keep more of your income working toward your million-dollar retirement goal, so you don't want to completely tap yourself out by taking the maximum allowed by a lender to apply to your mortgage. Some financial planners recommend using 20 percent of your gross income toward a monthly payment as your guide so you have money left over to meet your other financial and personal goals.

*"If you think education is expensive,
try ignorance."*
DEREK BOK

Long-term debt percentage

Now, the next factor lenders use to determine if you qualify for a particular loan is your long-term debt percentage. This percentage is calculated by dividing all of your debt obligations longer than ten months in duration (including your potential mortgage payment, car loans and any other credit) by your gross monthly income. For example, your gross monthly income is $5,000 and your gross monthly debt is $1,650. Your long-term debt percentage is 33 percent of $5,000. As a general rule, lenders don't want your long-term debt percentage to be more than 33 percent of your gross monthly income if your loan-to-value percentage is 90 percent. If your loan-to-value percentage is around 80 percent, they will allow your long-term debt percentage to be up to 36 percent of your gross monthly income. Again, it's better to move on the conservative side and keep your long-term debt percentage as low as possible. The lender may allow you to stretch and sweat each month, but that doesn't mean you have to *agree* to it.

Your mortgage amount

Now that you've computed these two factors to determine how much monthly mortgage payment you can afford, take a look at the table on page 136 from Griffeth to get an idea of the *total* mortgage you can afford.

Here's an example: You've done your figuring and you know you can afford an $850 monthly payment. (Figure 20 percent to 38 percent of gross monthly income to get your figure.) If the current interest rate for a 30-year fixed-rate mortgage is 7.5 percent, the chart on page 136 shows that you can afford a $122,000 loan.

This is simply a rough look at mortgage amounts and payments you can afford. "The actual amount you may be able to borrow will depend on among other things, the size of the down-payment you are willing to make and the amount of debt"[4] you have on your net-worth balance sheet.

HOW MUCH MORTGAGE CAN YOU AFFORD?

The Size Mortgage You Can Afford at These Interest Rates for a 30-Year Fixed-Rate Mortgage (in $Thousands)

Your Monthly Payment	6%	6.5%	7%	7.5%	8%	8.5%	9%
$400	$67	$62	$60	$57	$55	$52	$50
$450	$75	$72	$67	$65	$62	$57	$55
$500	$82	$80	$75	$72	$70	$65	$62
$550	$92	$87	$82	$77	$75	$72	$67
$600	$100	$95	$90	$87	$82	$77	$75
$650	$109	$105	$97	$92	$87	$85	$82
$700	$115	$111	$105	$100	$95	$92	$87
$750	$125	$119	$115	$107	$102	$97	$92
$800	$135	$127	$122	$115	$110	$105	$100
$850	$145	$135	$127	$122	$115	$112	$105
$900	$150	$145	$135	$127	$122	$118	$115
$950	$157	$150	$145	$135	$130	$122	$120
$1000	$167	$160	$150	$145	$137	$130	$125
$1100	$185	$175	$157	$152	$150	$145	$135
$1200	$200	$190	$180	$172	$165	$155	$150
$1300	$220	$215	$195	$185	$177	$170	$162
$1400	$235	$222	$215	$200	$190	$185	$175
$1500	$250	$237	$225	$218	$215	$195	$185

The downpayment

Once you decide the size of the mortgage you can afford, it's time to start figuring the downpayment you will need to save. Unlike saving for retirement, which is a long-term process, saving for a home downpayment has a shorter time-frame—probably three to five years. You may need to exercise every spending-less strategy you can think of to accomplish this short-term goal, but it's not an eternity of penny pinching—just a few years.

So how much will you need? The 20 percent goal is a good one to shoot for. When you place 20 percent down on a home, you don't have to add the expense of Private Mortgage Insurance (PMI), which lenders typically require on loans with anything less than a 20 percent downpayment. In general, PMI premiums usually run about .6 percent of the loan amount the first year and drop to about .5 percent in the following years. In addition to the extra monthly amount you'll have to pay to cover PMI, you'll also be asked to cover one full year of PMI premiums up front. So in our example of a $100,000 home loan, you will have to pay an added $50 a month for the PMI premium and add $600 up front to your closing costs. This whole PMI issue may get tricky, so pay attention here. If your bank loan doesn't mention PMI and you're putting only 10 percent down, watch out. The PMI may be hidden in the interest rate on the loan. If one bank is offering 7 percent with PMI for a fixed mortgage and your bank is offering you 7.6 percent without PMI, guess what— you're really paying for PMI even if it's not apparent. You may think it doesn't matter since the monthly figures work about the same. Wrong. PMI eventually goes away once you have built up 20 percent equity in your home. If you opted for the higher interest rate, you're stuck with it for the duration of the loan.

[*PMI note:* A law was passed in 1998 that required lenders to automatically cancel or notify borrowers of cancellation rights with respect to private mortgage insurance when borrowers reached the 20 percent equity mark. It is probably a good idea for you to track in your own records your progress toward this mark. If your lender does not cancel your PMI premium or notify you of your rights to do so, be sure to call your lender and eliminate this unnecessary expense.]

Saving your downpayment

So you've figured the size home you can afford, and you've figured the amount of downpayment you will need. Now the question to ask is, how do you save that amount? If you have a time-line of more than three years between now and when you plan to buy a home, you may want to consider building your downpayment in a *balanced* mutual fund (the kind that invests in equal parts blue-chip stocks and high-grade bonds). Also, in addition to the 20 percent you're saving for a downpayment, you will need to remember closing costs. Typically, as a buyer, you can expect to be charged 3 percent of the price of the house in closing costs. Obviously, the amount you pay in closing costs varies from state to state, so you may want to check this out with a lender before you begin the loan application process. Ask for a sample closing statement for a loan similar in amount to the one you're considering. A little research early on will prevent surprises later and give you a sense of peace about what to expect.

Burn date reminder

When you figure the amount of monthly payment you can afford, remember to consider your time-line between now and your goal to retire your home mortgage before you retire yourself. Figure in the extra principal payment in your affordability calculations. Ask your lender about the actual principal amount in the monthly payment and add that on to your monthly obligation to see if this is a loan you can afford and still meet your long-term goals.

Another angle

Here's a cool idea from financial consultant Henry Brock that will accomplish the same goal of living home-free at retirement.[5] This scenario will make the idea easier to understand. Assume you had a $209 difference between the 15-year mortgage and 30-year mortgage payment on a $100,000 loan. Let's also assume that a $100,000 term life insurance policy would cost you $20 a month in premiums. If you were to take that $209 plus the $20 term life premium and instead apply it to the purchase of a $100,000 permanent life insurance policy with cash value accumulations, here are the results. If the primary breadwinner were to die, the $100,000 death benefit could pay off the mortgage. But let's take the best scenario: the breadwinner lives and because the policy is accumulating cash on a tax-sheltered basis, this cash will build to the amount roughly equaling the remaining principal balance still owed on the home somewhere in year 15 to 17. Neat trick, right? Check it out with your insurance agent.

Due to sales tax and the fact you use after-tax dollars to buy things, you have to earn around $2 to cover $1 in spending.

BIDIA EMERGENCY FUNDING

Maybe you don't think you really need an emergency fund— after all, you have insurance, you have credit cards, you have discretionary dollars in your budget. Think again. Some financial experts say this is one of the most important steps you can take to securing your future. Bad things happen. Being prepared for when they do keeps you from having to tap into an investment at an unfavorable time or to sell valuables at fire-sale prices. Establishing a reserve account or emergency fund may not be uplifting or inspiring, but it's here in this chapter because you just need to do it anyway.

How much?

The formula to figure the amount you should sock away for rainy days varies from one financial consultant to another. Some say three to six months of your living expenses. Some say half of your annual income. Some say 10 percent of your annual income or $10,000, whichever is greater. You decide which sounds reasonable. The point is to set a goal and start building.

Should you build this emergency fund before you build your retirement? Should you build this emergency fund before you pay off your debt? Here was the general consensus out there in the world of financial advice. First, think in terms of setting aside 10 percent of your net income every month toward your financial goals. Keep this 10 percent goal firmly in mind each and every month. How you divide that 10 percent becomes a matter of priorities. Where should debt fall on this priority list? Experts say take it first! Pay it off with a vengeance. If you have to decide between a $10,000 emergency fund and paying off a credit card charging 18 percent interest, hit that card hard. Pay it off and then build your emergency account. After all, if you're faced with an emergency before you can build your reserve fund, you still have that card. After paying off your debt, you're faced with building an emergency fund, a retirement fund and possibly college funds. You can do all three at once by dividing your 10 percent again based on priorities. Focus on your reserve account for a few months until you have a cushion. Then shift your biggest percentage to your retirement fund. If you need to save for college funds, shift 2 percent in that direction and 8 percent toward retirement.

If you have your emergency cushion, and you're living true to the 10 percent rule for your future, congratulations! You're an exemplary member of the BIDIA club!

Four options to store emergency funds

Obviously, emergency funds need to be ready and waiting if the time comes when you need them. So what kinds of investments are out there that combine liquidity (can be turned into cash within 24 hours) and safety? Here are four options:

1. savings accounts
2. Certificates of Deposit (CDs)
3. Treasury Bills
4. money-market funds

A quick look at the upside and downside of these four options:

	The Good	The Bad
Savings account	is insured by government is immediately accessible	low return rate
Certificate of Deposit	is insured by government competitive rates	penalty if redeemed before maturity
Treasury Bills	liquid competitive rates	minimum purchase required; can lose some principal if sold before maturity date
Money-market account	liquid competitive rates	not insured

BIDIA INSURANCE DECISIONS

You're getting good at BIDIA decisions. You're living by a spending plan, you're building an emergency fund and now you're doing what's necessary to protect your family against financial disaster. This BIDIA activity involves choosing the right insurance plans to cover the catastrophes.

Catastrophe is a scary word. Most days don't include a catastrophe as part of the routine. The probability, in other words, for a catastrophe is low; however, the consequences could be devastating. Those are the conditions for insurance. The *only* conditions for insurance. In other words, insurance is for those things you can't afford to lose, and not for the small stuff. That means you can usually say "no thanks" to insurance such as:

- **Credit card insurance.** If you lose your card and call the credit card company before a fraudulent charge is made, you're not liable for paying that charge. If someone steals your card and charges the entire inventory of cashmere sweaters in Dillard's fall line and you don't notify the credit-card company, you are only liable for $50 of it. Instead of insurance, keep a list of your credit cards and phone numbers in your planner. (Debit cards operate under different rules. Check with your bank for specifics.)

- **Life or disability insurance tied to a specific debt.** Limited-purpose insurance such as mortgage insurance, credit life and credit disability are typically more expensive and more restrictive than plain term life or disability insurance.

- **Insurance that duplicates coverage you already have.** For example, health insurance for college students if they're on your existing policy, collision damage and personal articles insurance for rental cars if your auto insurance or credit-card company already covers you. Know what you have so you'll know what you don't need.

- **Insurance for a specific cause of death.** For example, flight insurance or cancer insurance or accidental death and dismemberment. You are typically much better off buying renewable term life insurance that covers you no matter how you die. A $250,000 20-year term life insurance policy for a 35-year-old non-smoking woman can cost less than $180 a year or $15 a month.

- **Life insurance on your children.** The purpose of life insurance is to protect dependents from the loss of a breadwinner. Unless your child is the breadwinner in your family, this is one insurance you can do without. If the agent tells you the plan is also a great way to save for college, check out the rate of return and compare it to a mutual fund. The better investment choice will be obvious.

Insure what you can't afford to replace; skip the insurance on the small stuff.

INSURANCE YOU DO NEED

Here are the essentials as recommended by the experts: health insurance, automobile insurance, disability insurance and life insurance, in most cases. Let's take the high points of each one:

Health insurance

No need to talk about why this one is necessary. No doubt you've experienced the value of health insurance firsthand. So let's just move into the considerations that affect you as a self-employed individual. The IRS has given you a break in two ways when it comes to health insurance. First, the medical savings account program is designed for the self-employed person. The idea is this: Let's say you want to cut down on health insurance premiums so you raise your deductible to $2,000 for an individual and $5,000 for your family. Here's where the medical savings account comes in. You are allowed to keep up to 65 percent of the deductible for yourself, or up to 75 percent if you have a family, in a medical savings account. You can deduct the full amount of your contribution to the account from your income-tax return. The sum in your account grows tax-deferred to age 65. If you have to tap into the account for medical reasons at any time, no tax is due on what you use. If you use it for any other reason, yes, you pay income tax plus a 15 percent penalty. This program could likely change over time. Watch for the latest on the news or ask your accountant or tax adviser.

Protect your family by having adequate life insurance on yourself and your husband, not on the children.

Another tax break for the self-employed may make buying your health insurance a better deal than having a medical savings account. Under the Tax and Trade Relief Extension Act of 1998, the deductions for health insurance expenses of self-employed persons (and family members) will steadily rise to 100 percent in 2003.

This hefty deduction could be a nice bite out of your income-tax bill. Also, be sure to check out group rates for health insurance available to self-employed individuals through professional groups and organizations. Health insurance is an area that is in constant flux. No one knows what health insurance coverage will be like when our children are shopping around for policies. Stay awake on this one. Watch for changes and research all new possibilities. Health insurance is a must for living rich in peace of mind and financial security. Make it a priority on your insurance list of must-haves.

Disability insurance

You may have a tendency to just glance at this type of insurance, but take a second look. A 35-year-old has about a one in three chance of becoming disabled for at least six months before reaching age 65. The issue to consider here is whether your family could sustain itself financially if you or your husband stopped working due to an illness or accident. If the answer is "no," then you may want to take the advice of the experts and start shopping for disability insurance. Many employers offer disability coverage, so if your husband is employed, ask him to check into it. Also, check with a licensed insurance agent for appropriate coverage for you.

The cost of this insurance will vary depending on your age, sex, occupation and policy features. Here are the features that you will need to consider when shopping for disability insurance:

- **Benefit period.** Some policies are short-term and pay benefits for up to two years. Others pay benefits until age 65 if you are permanently disabled. Obviously, the shorter the benefit term, the lower the premium.

- **Waiting period.** This is how long you wait after becoming disabled before benefits kick in. Your choices are typically 30, 60, 90, 120 or 180 days. The longer the wait, the lower the premium.

- **Definition of disability.** Some policies dictate that you are disabled if you're unable to continue doing your usual work. Others say you're disabled only if you can't work at all. The more liberal the definition, the higher the premium.

- **Residual benefits.** Some policies don't have a residual benefit clause, which means your benefits would cease if you went back to work part-time after becoming disabled.

- **Renewability and noncancellability.** A guaranteed renewable, noncancellable policy means as long as you pay the premiums, the insurer can't cancel your policy. Most issuers will cancel the policy, however, once you reach the age when you can collect Social Security benefits.

- **Cost-of-living escalator.** This feature protects you against the erosion of your benefits due to inflation. Benefits are automatically adjusted according to the rate of inflation. The younger you are, the more important this feature is.

- **Waiver of premium.** With this feature, if you become disabled, your premiums stop during the period of disability.

Automobile insurance

If you have purchased your car on credit, then by all means have collision and damage coverage (required by most lenders). Remember, the rule of thumb is to cover what you can't afford to replace. Then, in all circumstances be sure you have liability coverage to protect you if anyone sues because they've been injured in or by your car.

Car insurance premiums are all over the ballpark. To make sure you're getting the best price for the best coverage, you may want to check out the *Consumer Reports* auto insurance price comparison line at 1-800-807-8050. For a small fee, *Consumer Reports* will analyze 175 different policies to find the right policy to fit your needs, send you a customized six-page report listing up to 25 of the lowest-priced policies, and provide tips and advice about how to save money on auto insurance. Unfortunately, this service isn't available in all states, so check to see if your state is included. If you call and your state isn't covered, the representative will refer you to the issue of *Consumer Reports* in which automobile insurance is featured. You may also want to contact your state's Department of Insurance. This department will provide such information as satisfaction ratings on specific companies. This is a big chunk out of your monthly budget, so take the time to do your homework. You may be able to shave off enough on this one expense to help fund your emergency or retirement accounts.

Life insurance

I know it's easy to glaze over when you hear "life insurance." There's just nothing snazzy about this topic. However, remember the neat trick of using a cash-value life insurance to pay off a mortgage in case of a death or prepay the mortgage with the accumulated cash? Or remember the strategy of using life insurance to replace the inheritance to your children when you use a charitable remainder trust in estate planning? Life insurance is an incredibly smart tool to use in your financial plan. And, of course, there's the most obvious benefit of life insurance—the benefit that comes to the people who depend on you should you leave them while they still need your financial support.

So let's take a quick course in the basics of life insurance. Essentially, there are two over-arching types of life insurance:

Term insurance

Term insurance covers you for a specific term instead of your whole life. There are no cash accumulations—strictly a death benefit applicable to a specific length of time. The advantage of term insurance is the lower premium. You can secure the same dollar amount of insurance for a much lower premium with term life insurance. Many people who buy term insurance set the term of coverage for the length of time it takes to raise their children and get them through college.

When shopping for term life insurance, a basic understanding of your choices is a good idea. Here is the gist of it: There are two kinds of term life insurance—annually renewable term and level premium term. If you choose annually renewable term insurance, your premium goes up every year because statistically you're more likely to die as you get older. Logical, right? Level premium term insurance costs more each year initially, but the premiums stay consistent for the term you've established. You also don't have to go through the process of renewing your policy each year, which could be wise if you should become ill.

Cash-value insurance

The next category of life insurance falls under the umbrella of cash-value insurance. Cash-value policies cost more than term policies and provide more. Actually, you get two things with a cash-value policy—a death benefit as with traditional life insurance, plus a variety of savings, investment and payment options. A portion of the premium you pay secures the life insurance; the rest of your premium is put into an account where it grows on a tax-deferred basis. Variations on this theme come in the way of whole life, universal life and variable life.

To give you a simple overview of what you can expect in premiums, take a look at this chart supplied by the National Insurance Consumer Organization.

YEARLY PREMIUMS FOR A $100,000 POLICY			
Age	Term Insurance	Universal Life Insurance	Whole-life Insurance
30	$ 136	$ 590	$ 875
35	140	746	1,095
40	163	950	1,391
45	205	1,217	1,776
50	320	1,583	2,311
55	440	2,078	3,038
60	610	2,741	4,717
65	980	3,665	5,376

LONG-TERM CARE

Although long-term care insurance doesn't fall into the "must-have" category, it is becoming more and more important for a strong financial plan. We are living longer. That's good, of course, but it also accounts for the fact that more and more of us will need long-term care at some point in our lives. According to Michael Snowden, an academic associate at the College for Financial Planners, the American Health Care Association conducted a study that found one in three of those who reach 65 years of age will spend some time in a nursing home, and one in four will spend a year or longer. The average nursing home stay is 2-½ years at around $40,000 a year.

So how do you pay for it if you are the one in four? A common misconception is that Medicare or a Medicare supplemental insurance will pay for long-term care. Here are the facts: Medicare does not cover care in a skilled nursing facility beyond 100 days per benefit period nor does it cover custodial care in your home. Medicare supplements don't substantially expand that coverage. Then there's Medicaid. Medicaid covers long-term nursing home stays and sometimes home health care, but you basically have to be impoverished before qualifying for coverage.

So your best option? A long-term care insurance policy if you fit this scenario: The United Seniors Health Cooperative says that long-term care insurance is a good option for households

In general, it doesn't make sense to purchase long-term care insurance for yourself until you are in your mid- to late 50s.

with more than $75,000 in assets per person, income of $30,000 or more per person and the ability to afford premium increases of 20 percent to 30 percent in the future. If you have less than these assets and income, the organization says you may find coverage too expensive and it may be better to rely on other options.

If you opt for long-term care insurance from a private insurance company, the policies vary greatly, so shop around and read the fine print. Each policy will have its own eligibility requirements, restrictions, costs and benefits. Here are the basic questions to ask when comparing policies:

1. Are there any conditions I must meet to collect the benefits?

2. Will the policy pay for home care or hospice care?

3. Does the benefit amount increase over time to keep up with inflation?

4. Will any coverage be provided if my policy lapses in future years?

5. How long has this company been in the business of long-term care insurance? (Experts recommend at least eight years in business.)

6. What is the company rating? (Experts suggest you accept nothing less than an A-rated company.)

Since entering into an insurance agreement requires the insurance company to be around when you need it, taking the time to investigate the financial stability of a company and its past performance in service is a wise idea. Here is a sampling of rating companies and their numbers:

1. Duff & Phelps   312-368-3100
2. Standard & Poor's 212-438-2000
3. Weiss Research   800-289-9222

Weiss charges a small fee for ratings; however, it may be worth it since it is known for being conservative and tough in its ratings. This is one of the few rating companies that is not supported or affiliated with insurance companies. Its ratings are totally independent for the benefit of the consumer.

LESSON IN THE IMPORTANCE OF INSURANCE

*M*y husband and I have had several reasons to think about the importance of long-term care insurance. My mother came to live with us for four years while she had cancer. After six months in the hospital, her health insurance stopped paying. My dad passed away during the time my mom was in the hospital. My Mary Kay income played a huge role in my mother's care. My mom died in 1983. Then six years ago, my father-in-law was diagnosed with cancer and my husband John cared for him. After my father-in-law and then my mother-in-law passed away (they passed away within five months of each other), John's sister, who has cerebral palsy, came to live with us for five years. Now she's living independently in her own apartment with a roommate. It's obvious we've had reasons to think of long-term care. Another insurance must-have is disability insurance. John had a heart attack a few years ago and now has a built-in defibrillator. It would have been quite difficult for us financially if it weren't for John's disability insurance.

— JUDY KAWIECKI, Independent Executive Senior Sales Director

When should you buy long-term care insurance?

Experts say the most cost-effective time for you to consider purchasing a long-term insurance policy is when you reach your mid- to late 50s. However, even if you're younger, long-term care is an important consideration for you if you have parents. Statistics show that an estimated 43 percent of current senior citizens will spend time in a nursing home. If your parents' assets (excluding their home and car) are valued at less than $50,000, you can probably skip over long-term care insurance from a private company. It's probably not worth the cost. If, however, your parents' assets are relatively substantial, and they want to pass an inheritance on to you and your children, a long-term care policy may be a good idea.

How much does long-term care insurance cost?

Based on the American Council of Life Insurance, here is a rough idea of what you can expect in premiums:

AVERAGE ANNUAL PREMIUMS		
Ages	2-Year Policy	5-Year Policy
35–39	$394	$558
40–44	443	666
45–49	550	807
50–54	645	905
55–59	892	1,204
60–64	1,265	1,709
65–69	1,849	2,432
70–74	2,638	3,610
75+	3,851	5,274

Six Most Important Things to Do to Join the BIDIA Club:

1. Record your every expense for three months.

2. Transfer your spending decisions to a monthly cash-flow sheet. It's a good idea to repeat this process every month.

3. Create a budget based on a give-and-save-first, spend-later model. Cut spending in order to make that model a reality.

4. If you don't own a home, evaluate that possibility. Figure what you could afford and how much you would need to save. The simple act of going through this process will take you closer to realizing home ownership.

5. Build an emergency fund in the amount of 10 percent of your annual income or $10,000—whichever is greater.

6. Secure insurance to cover everything you can't afford to replace. Insurance essentials are: life insurance if you have dependents, health insurance, disability income insurance and liability insurance on your car and property.

Definitions of Living Rich

The ability to help my family financially and emotionally.
—*Judi Tapella*

Of course it's having the money to satisfy our wants and needs,
but it extends to the quality of our lives as well.
—*Alicia Wilson*

Being balanced, stress-free and abundantly free from
a monotonous daily life.
—*Vicki Auth*

Being able to help others, church, colleges, family members
and, most of all, to be able to invest freely.
—*Joyce C. Revere*

Helping my children get ready for life.
—*Kathy Wickler*

Seeing my children learn about Europe by walking in Europe
instead of reading about it in the encyclopedia.
—*Elaine Garner*

Having the freedom of time and money to enjoy
my family and build memories together.
—*Margaret Baggett*

Choices, choices, choices.
—*Stephanie Bowen*

Having my marriage intact and in full bloom after 35 years.
—*Jeannette Alexander*

Travelling to "exotic" places!
—*Julie Garrison*

Living a Rich Life

CHAPTER SEVEN

Law #1: Team Up

I believe that everybody who accomplishes something great had help from someone. Somebody, somewhere provided a spark of inspiration, offered a challenge or held out a hand along the way. The wonderful feeling that comes from helping people gives meaning to your accomplishments. If you don't help others, your own success means less; it may even feel hollow. — M A R Y   K A Y   A S H

I WAS RECENTLY INVITED TO PARTICIPATE in a meeting of the "Helping Women Team" at Mary Kay headquarters. The simple fact that there *is* such a team at a billion-dollar corporation is impressive in its own right. But as I sat there and felt the passion in the hearts of the team members and heard the dedication and personal commitments to the mission of Mary Kay to help women no matter who they were, where they were or what their need— I knew this was a company that lived the words of its mission statement.

Then I heard a story that made it all so real to me. I heard how a Mary Kay Beauty Consultant's daughter who was stricken with cancer needed a particular drug to raise her platelet level high enough to allow her to undergo chemotherapy. The problem was that this young lady lived in Argentina where the drug would not be available for several months. Of course, she needed it *now*. Instead of a "how sad" attitude, the Mary Kay Ash Charitable Foundation went into action and helped secure an import license for the drug from the Argentinian government agency within two hours. The drug was shipped immediately.

Teamwork at its zenith! Partnering like this makes working not seem like working at all. Success becomes even more wonderful, which is exactly what Mary Kay Ash had in mind. She structured her Company around teamwork—growth in your business is the result of building relationships, extending a helping hand, coming together toward a common goal. The effects of teamwork on the economics and emotional satisfaction of your business is obvious.

But what about in your family? How does teamwork in your family affect your finances? That's the subject of this chapter—the economic benefits of teaming up with your husband, teaming up with your children, and teaming up with aging parents; in other words, how embracing one another will bring new meaning to your success and stability to your finances.

We'll start with your hubby—how to make yours and mine turn into a bigger pot of "ours." Next, we'll talk about how your children play a role in the process and how to make them more aware, more respectful and more likely to be money-savvy adults. And finally, we'll take a look at the special money concerns you face when it comes to aging parents.

*Teams bring together complementary skills
that exceed those of any individual on
the team. 1 + 1 = 3*

Financial consultant Henry S. Brock[1] refers to the family as "the most efficient economic unit in our society." If that statement seems like a stretch, this may be an important chapter for you. Embrace it, then embrace one another and enjoy the feeling!

Your hubby and money

How many times has the subject of money come up in your conversations with your husband? If you're like most couples, the topic is a constant. Money usually plays a powerful role in relationships. It may not buy happiness, but it sure seems to buy plenty of disagreements. Maybe a close look at money and marriage will help you avoid the heated debates that snare so many couples.

PREPARE FOR A PRENUPTIAL CONVERSATION

First, let's take a step back and look at the discussion you *should* have had *before* the ceremony. Maybe that's history for you, but remember there are plenty of women out there who may need this advice. So if you're married, pass it on. If you're not, soak it up! According to financial consultant Jill Gianola,[2] there are five top money questions to include in a prenuptial conversation. Here are her five questions, along with our elaboration on each one:

1. **"What does your balance sheet look like?"** If you are signing a prenuptial agreement, obviously both of you need to look at a full disclosure of assets and liabilities. Even if you're skipping the prenup, a sharing of a balance sheet (net-worth statement) is a good idea. A negative net worth may be a sign of trouble. Of course, consider the situation. If your partner-to-be has just finished medical school and has a hefty student loan on the liability side, that's a far different story than when liability is made up of credit-card debt and car loans.

2. **"What is your credit rating?"** Maybe a better idea than asking this question is exchanging your credit reports. This is a great time to review your own credit rating while checking into your future partner's. Why do you care about his credit rating? Joint purchases you make together, as in the case of a house, will be affected by his credit rating. A poor rating may mean a higher interest rate or a smaller mortgage. In any case, looking at a credit report is a great way to get a little insight into how your future mate handles debt.

3. **"Do you want children?"** Obviously having children is more than a financial decision, but because it has such huge money ramifications, we'll add it to this money discussion. The two of you should discuss how you'll handle raising children. Will both of you continue to work? What kind of child care do you envision?

4. **"How was money handled when you were growing up?"** Adult attitudes about money are often created in your parents' home. If gifts were used by your parents to show love, spending money on someone may represent affection to you as an adult. If extreme financial hardships were a part of your early years, a tight-fisted response to money may be the norm now. Having a heart-to-heart about the past is a sure way to get a better picture of the future.

5. **"What are your financial goals?"** Taking the long-term view with a future partner is important. Ask about retirement. What is his dream? What does he think is the ideal career? Does he feel parents should completely fund their children's educations? What about home ownership? Then move on to the everyday issues—how does he feel about budgeting? Tracking spending? Saving for emergencies?

If your future spouse has children from a previous marriage, Jill Gianola suggests you add these questions to your list:[3]

- "What are your ongoing financial responsibilities regarding alimony and child support?

- How much do you spend on your children? What do they expect? Have they been promised a new car at graduation and full payment of college bills?"

Certainly this is a tough topic to bring up as you sip lemonade on the front porch swing, but find the courage. Love and marriage is about more than playing kissy-face in the moonlight. It's about teamwork—in the good times and the bad, and money is usually a part of both. So have this discussion and give your marriage a firm grounding.

UNDERSTAND YOUR DIFFERENCES

The next step in avoiding the money traps in marriage is to understand the typical differences men and women have about money. Financial consultant Ginita Wall[4] points out three primary differences. Here is her list of differences along with our elaboration on each:

1. **"Different fears"** A lot of women, regardless of income level, have a nagging fear that no matter how much they have now, it could someday all disappear. Psychologists call this the bag-lady syndrome.

   Men, on the other hand, don't fear this kind of general onslaught of poverty. They tend to think in terms of specific events that could change their financial situation, such as getting injured and being unable to work or getting laid off and unable to find a new job. Their concerns revolve around letting down their family, not sleeping in a shopping cart under a bridge.

2. **"Different approaches"** Women tend to manage money using a combination of logic and intuition. Men are more likely to make money decisions based on advice from friends.

    Also, women aren't intimidated by asking questions. As a result, we ask questions before we do anything with our money. Men, on the other hand, well, you've probably ridden with a man who didn't know where he was going. Did he ask? Usually not—he's so predictable about not asking, the whole scenario has become a cliché. Apply that same approach to money matters, and you get the picture. In general, men like to appear to know it all, whether they are behind the wheel of a car or online with a broker.

3. **"Different goals"** Women may see retirement as the perfect time to build a business. Men may see it as a time to kick back, watch a little football and play golf three times a week. It's not unusual for men and women to have conflicting retirement dreams.

That brief overview of male and female differences regarding money has been for one purpose—to make you more determined than ever to sit down and talk with your husband about how the two of you line up on money. Money is a charged subject. It doesn't matter how much or how little of it you have, how you handle it can enrage the calmest soul and build a wedge between the closest partners.

Opposites may attract, but different money styles can cause serious conflicts. Talk about money styles and try to move to more neutral positions.

HAVE A HEART-TO-HEART

So the next step in your quest to merge marriage and money is sit down together and talk about money views and attitudes. According to Olivia Mellan,[5] money therapist and author of *Money Harmony: Resolving Money Conflicts in Your Life and Relationships*, there are definite ways to make your discussion about money attitudes more constructive. Here is the gist of her ideas:

1. **Make sure you schedule your discussions at calm times.** In other words, don't expect a healthy, exploratory money exchange while you're in the middle of filing your income tax or sitting down with a pile of bills to pay.

2. **Allow one another the freedom to talk without interruptions.** Even if you don't agree with what's being said, the simple act of sharing and listening will do wonders for building a healthy money relationship.

3. **Reveal your innermost desires and fears and be sure not to criticize your partner when he does the same. This is no time to drag out a past credit-card statement and start pointing fingers.** Listen as if you are having your first cup of coffee with this guy and you are truly interested in getting beneath the surface.

4. **Share your goals about your future.** Do you see yourself scaling down in retirement and buying a condo or building your dream house? Share with your husband the goals you established in Chapter 2. Tell him what you feel is your purpose in life. Share with him the legacy you want to leave. Tell him when you want to be financially independent. Ask him to share the same with you. Then plan together how much money you will need to make those dreams and goals come true. Crunch the numbers. Make it a buddy-plan.

5. **Keep what you learn in this discussion pure and positive.** Don't use any part of it as fire-power during your next money argument.

ASSUAGE THE RAGE

If after having this heart-to-heart with your husband about money, you still experience times you question if this man standing before you is actually *of* this universe, you may want to try Olivia Mellan's approaches to ease money conflicts:

1. **Walk a mile in his shoes.** Let's just say your money styles are different. *Your* greatest joy is opening your investment report and seeing your balance move upward. *His* is coming home from Circuit City with the latest electronic gizmo in his hand and a charge slip in his pocket. What do a spender and a saver do to reconcile their differences and live happily ever after? Mellan suggests trying role reversal. The spender could take 5 percent of the next paycheck and invest it into an account. The saver could take 5 percent and buy a personal gift or one for someone else. Trying on your partner's money style, even if only for a short time, will help you develop a greater understanding of his feelings and how your habits probably make him a little crazy.

2. **Admit to the things about his style that you like.** Maybe there's something free-spirited about your partner's spending style that you secretly admire. You haven't told him so for fear he will go on a spending spree out of sheer exhilaration of your confession. Maybe a spender secretly admires the self-control shown by the saving partner. Nothing has been said, of course, for fear a tighter budget could result. Open up and reveal these undercurrents of admiration. It just may be the catalyst for agreement that helps you move more closely to each other's style.

3. **Move to a more neutral zone.** You are who you are. Your husband is who he is. You can, however, become more flexible about your choices if you understand your styles and make a com-

mitment to move extreme positions more toward middle ground. Money worriers could tell themselves to commit their worries to paper instead of in their spouses' ears and then let their worries go for the rest of the day. Money avoiders could commit to doing what they typically avoid, such as balancing their checkbooks as soon as the bank statement comes in. Then when you've made a step toward the middle, reward yourselves with a hug and warm smile.

Here is another idea that may help a coming-together on money issues: create mine, yours and ours accounts.

If both you and your spouse are entirely practical, with a frugal mentality overriding the importance of personal freedom, one bank account shared between the two of you may fit your styles beautifully. And as a bonus, you'll have only one service charge each month instead of two. However, if that arrangement feels a little cramped and restrictive, you may want to consider the advice of a great many financial advisers and have three accounts—a yours, a mine and an ours account. It works like this: You each have a checking account along with one joint account into which each of you contributes a set amount each month to pay joint expenses (discussed in Chapter 6). If you have a joint expense beyond the bounds of your budget, you treat it separately by putting extra money in the joint account that month or writing a check from your personal accounts to cover your portion of the purchase. The money you have left in your personal accounts should be "no-questions-asked" money. What he does with *his* is his business. What you do with *yours* is your business.

The added bonus of this arrangement is avoiding what Debtors Anonymous calls "terminal vagueness." With one account many times no single person feels ultimately responsible for what's happening. Each person has a false sense of security. They each feel protected by the existence of the other. Women especially have fallen into this trap of feeling "safe" when they're sharing accounts with their husbands. The stability of family finance depends on the stability of each of you as individuals. Dual accounts make it clear who is doing what, when and how much.

*Be sure to contribute to your own
retirement plan instead of focusing entirely
on your husband's plan. Also, be sure not to balance
your family investments by using your plan
to offset your husband's—that is, by putting all your
savings into a conservative, lower-earnings investment
while your husband places his funds in riskier,
higher-earnings investments. Each spouse's retirement
plan should be balanced individually.*

LESSON IN TEAMING UP WITH HUBBY

I was earning over $100,000 per year in commissions from my Mary Kay business before I was 30 years old. Although I invested in some rental property, I'm sorry to say I did not build a portfolio. Then I met my husband, who is a stockbroker. Today we laugh about the first time he asked me out on the premise of talking to me about investments but never opened his portfolio. Since then, however, we've developed systems to handle our joint finances. I take money out monthly to place in my SEP account. It comes right off the top. He has his own retirement plan with his company. We have tithes, which are important to us because we can place money where we feel the Lord is leading. In addition to my business account, we have three checking accounts. We divide up the household expenses and split the financial responsibility. We have an incidental spending account which we place money in each month. This money we use for gifts, clothing and little things that come up. We do this so we're not charging on credit cards. Then we have two other checking accounts. One is what I call a "holding" account. I use it to hold money I've collected from people to pay for meetings and other expenses. By placing the money in this special account, when the bill comes, I have the money to pay it. Then I have what I call a "stash" account. I put bonuses in this account so I have several thousand dollars handy for special purchases—things like vacations and special gifts for family members. I also use this account to pay my quarterly estimated tax payments. The phrase, "If you don't manage your money, it will manage you" is really true. When thinking about money styles for my husband and me, I have to say that we are more alike today than we once were. I used to look at my Mary Kay income for what it could buy instead of how it could be invested to multiply and to create a secure future. Now, we have a basic feeling about money that's common to both of us. We respect money for the choices it gives us. We can send our children to the best schools and we can enjoy a lifestyle that's peaceful and secure. As an Independent National Sales Director, we don't have to choose between enjoying extras and savings. I feel blessed to be able to do both. There's an important value in shifting your money style to investing for the future. **—ALIA HEAD, Independent National Sales Director**

AVOID COMMON MISTAKES

According to the Women's Institute for a Secure Retirement,[6] a lot of women in couples make the same mistakes. Here is their list of the most common ones along, with our comments:

1. **"Not getting involved in managing the family's finances."** Of course, just one of you will write the checks for joint expenses. Who does is really unimportant. What does matter is that both of you are making the decisions together. Be sure you know where all your money is invested—yours and his. Also, keep up with the value of each of these investments.

2. **"Using your money for everyday expenses"** . . . while your husband's money goes into investments. Both of you should contribute fairly to buying groceries and school supplies for the kids.

3. **"Trying to pay for half of everything when you really can't afford it."** Remember the fair percentage concept discussed in Chapter 6? Fair is fair. Keep it that way so you'll have money for your own savings and investment plans.

4. **"Not getting professional advice soon enough."** Before you make any big moves in your life, you need to find out right away the financial ramifications of your decisions. Don't hesitate to ask an expert.

5. **"Not realizing that you may end up living on your own someday."** Unfortunately, many marriages end in divorce. Also, statistically women live longer than men. It makes sense to prepare to manage your own finances. Make sure your name is on all family accounts and investments alongside your husband's in order to establish your legal rights.

Your kids and money

When it comes to teaching kids how to live a rich life, we have to think in terms of character first. No one is truly rich if he or she lacks character. Teaching children to honor themselves by being honest, to be tolerant of differences, to be kind to all living things, to be compassionate in times of distress and giving in times of need—these are lessons that build character. Teaching children the essence of the Golden Rule—what they give out will eventually return to them—is a lesson to build character. Teaching children that all which is of this earth is of God and deserves their respect and courteous goodwill—this is a lesson to build character. You know these lessons well. We were taught by example in the life of Mary Kay Ash. Use these lessons every day as you interact with your children, for it's in the quiet daily acts that habits will develop. Habits, in turn, develop character and character ultimately is the answer to living rich.

TEACH THEM ABOUT PERSISTENCE

The one character-building lesson that stands tall among the rest when it comes to creating wealth is the lesson of persistence. If you allow your child to quit the soccer team because the going is getting tough, that little act of quitting carves out the beginning of a habit. What happens later? Quitting college? Quitting a job? Maybe quitting a marriage? Any one of these grown-up acts of giving up has devastating economic consequences. Not to mention the emotional blows. Mary Kay Ash once said that a determined person cannot be kept from success . . . no matter what. Instill this lesson. Coming home from camp early because the temperature was "just too hot," dropping out of an honor's class because the standards were "just too high" or dumping a friend at a moment's notice because she expected "just too much"—there's no persistence here. Teach an attitude of hanging in there a bit longer. Remember the 18-year-old who became a millionaire through the dollar-a-day investment habit? Quitting on that commitment during those 49 years would have been much easier. Persistence, however, created wealth.

Give your children the encouragement to keep going when things get tough. Help them understand that difficulty is to be expected. It's not an excuse to quit. It's a reason to grow— personally and financially.

Connect with your children with a different kind of vacation. If your children are old enough, think about volunteering as a family. Look into working for Habitat for Humanity (www.habitat.org) or helping the Red Cross (www.redcross.org). Volunteers usually cover their own expenses, so check your budget and be sure this idea works for you.

TEACH THEM ABOUT CASH FLOW

Most children never really see the bills or your commission checks or your husband's paycheck. It's all some vague mystery. Maybe it's time they had a realistic picture of what earning and living is all about. Try this one month: Cash your checks and pile the money on the dining room table. Then take all your bills for the month and place them around the table. Divide the necessary money up to pay each bill and stack the money on top of the appropriate bill. Be sure to include your giving choices and your savings and investment accounts right along with your bills.

Now your children will actually see how money comes in and money goes out. They may be a little more sensitive to your situation when you say "not now" to their next gotta-have-it request.

TEACH THEM ABOUT SAVING AND INVESTING

Financial consultants advise a hands-on approach when teaching saving and investing to children. Instead of handing out money whenever a want or need pops up, allow your child to furnish the dollars required. That means establishing a method for the child to earn cash and make decisions with that cash. You may want to have three jars in your child's room. One jar is marked "For Things I Want Now." The second jar is labeled "For Things I Want Soon." The third jar is labeled "For Things I Want Later." The child then allocates his or her allowance according to these three designations. Daily spending money is in the first jar. Funds to save for things like a new bike or skateboard are in the second jar. And money to build toward maybe a car or special camp is in the third jar. Stick a picture of the desired "big" goals in the appropriate jars to inspire determination when the days get long.

When your child gets a little older, you may want to transfer the jar idea into savings and investment accounts. That second jar becomes a savings account at your local bank. The third jar becomes a mutual fund if the long-term goal is at least three years away. The money then has a greater chance of growing into the sum needed to reach the goal.

Explain the difference between the jar and the investment account to your child. A very simple example of compounding will probably do the trick to convince your child the investment account makes sense. Here is an easy one: Ask your child which he would prefer—$1,000 a day for 30 days *or* a penny the first day, two cents the next, four cents the next and doubling that penny amount every day thereafter for a total of 30 days. Ask which option is better. Then show your child the results of each. The charts included here from Bill Griffeth's book, *10 Steps to Financial Prosperity,*[7] will clearly show the magic of compounding and the wisdom of an investment account over a jar.

THE MAGIC OF COMPOUNDING		
	Payment	Cumulative Total
Day 1	$1,000	$1,000
Day 2	$1,000	$2,000
Day 3	$1,000	$3,000
Day 4	$1,000	$4,000
Day 5	$1,000	$5,000
Day 6	$1,000	$6,000
Day 7	$1,000	$7,000
Day 8	$1,000	$8,000
Day 9	$1,000	$9,000
Day 10	$1,000	$10,000
Day 11	$1,000	$11,000
Day 12	$1,000	$12,000
Day 13	$1,000	$13,000
Day 14	$1,000	$14,000
Day 15	$1,000	$15,000
Day 16	$1,000	$16,000
Day 17	$1,000	$17,000
Day 18	$1,000	$18,000
Day 19	$1,000	$19,000
Day 20	$1,000	$20,000
Day 21	$1,000	$21,000
Day 22	$1,000	$22,000
Day 23	$1,000	$23,000
Day 24	$1,000	$24,000
Day 25	$1,000	$25,000
Day 26	$1,000	$26,000
Day 27	$1,000	$27,000
Day 28	$1,000	$26,000
Day 29	$1,000	$29,000
Day 30	$1,000	$30,000

Being paid $1,000 a day for 30 days obviously results in $30,000. Starting off with one penny a day, with a doubling of the previous day's total thereafter for 30 days, results in a total of $10,737,418.23. That's the benefit of compounding—reinvesting dividends and interest so your dollars grow over time.

THE MAGIC OF COMPOUNDING		
	Payment	**Cumulative Total**
Day 1	$.01	$.01
Day 2	$.02	$.03
Day 3	$.04	$.07
Day 4	$.08	$.15
Day 5	$.16	$.31
Day 6	$.32	$.63
Day 7	$.64	$1.27
Day 8	$1.28	$2.55
Day 9	$2.56	$5.11
Day 10	$5.12	$10.23
Day 11	$10.24	$20.47
Day 12	$20.48	$40.95
Day 13	$40.96	$81.91
Day 14	$81.92	$163.83
Day 15	$163.84	$327.67
Day 16	$327.68	$655.35
Day 17	$655.36	$1,310.71
Day 18	$1,310.72	$2,621.43
Day 19	$2,621.44	$5,242.87
Day 20	$5,242.88	$10,485.75
Day 21	$10,485.76	$20,971.51
Day 22	$20,971.52	$41,943.03
Day 23	$41,943.04	$83,886.07
Day 24	$83,886.08	$167,772.15
Day 25	$167,772.16	$335,544.31
Day 26	$335,544.32	$671,088.63
Day 27	$671,088.64	$1,342,177.27
Day 28	$1,342,177.28	$2,684,354.55
Day 29	$2,684,354.56	$5,368,709.11
Day 30	$5,368,709.12	$10,737,418.23

Also, a quick explanation of the Rule of 72 may be a good lesson to teach concerning investments. By dividing the interest rate you're receiving into 72, you get the number of years it takes to double your money. For example, with a 10 percent return, it will take approximately 7.2 years to double your money ($72 \div 10 = 7.2$). There's no doubling effect in the jar no matter how many years you leave it there.

After you've helped your child establish an investment fund, celebrate the quarterly statements together. Look at that ending balance and compare it with the last one you received. What a great way to prepare your child to think long term, value persistence and understand the opportunity that comes from making an investment choice over a spending choice!

TEACH THEM ABOUT CREDIT

Next comes the credit-card discussion. Credit-card companies have a new market—your teenage child. It's common for college students and even seniors in high school to be swamped with credit-card solicitations. Even though this new market rarely has income, it's a good risk because the parents of under-18 teenagers must cosign their loans and stand behind their debts.

There's an upside and downside to this mix of credit cards and teenagers. On the upside, a student who uses a credit card will graduate from college with an established credit rating, which makes renting a first apartment or buying a car an easier task. The downside only comes into play if your child doesn't pay the bills on time. A child under 18 can't get a card without a cosigner, and when an adult cosigns, that adult becomes legally obligated to pay the bills. To weaken the limb you're standing on, the lender is not obligated to notify the cosigner even if the loan goes into default. And here's a scary thought: Once that student turns 19, he or she can get multiple cards and once the bills are beginning to be paid, issuers will increase the credit line.

It's not inconceivable that by the time your freshman turns into a sophomore in college, he or she could possibly have up to $25,000 in charging capacity.

So what do you do? Gerri Detweiler, author of the audiocassette *Smart Credit Strategies for College Students,*[8] suggests this: Pick one credit card on which you are the primary borrower and your child is the cosigner. As a cosigner, your child will build a credit history, but as the primary borrower, you'll get the statements. No surprises. You can keep an eye on the process. Here are a few other tips adapted from Detweiler's work:

1. **Help your children learn to use credit wisely well before they head off to college.** Start their education around the age of 15. Teach them by using your own credit experiences. Go over your credit-card statements so they see the complete picture of a credit-card purchase. Explain how finance charges, grace periods, minimum payments and late fees work. Give them an example of how frighteningly fast a balance can grow if they make only minimum payments as they accumulate new charges (more in Chapter 9).

2. **Explain why credit-card companies are so eager to get your child's business.** Describe how, from the very first purchase on the card, the credit bureaus will be watching the account. Explain that late payments will show on the child's credit report for seven years—and that information could hurt their chances of buying a car, renting an apartment or getting a first mortgage in the future.

3. **Agree on limits—how the card is to be used and for what kinds of purchases.** If it is an "emergency only" card, explain that pizza and a snazzy new pair of jeans are not emergencies. If the card is for general purchases, set a monthly limit. Make it clear you won't pay for items beyond this limit unless they are preapproved by you.

The bottom line is this: If you teach your children to capitalize on the power of investing, to respect the use of credit cards and to appreciate the potential of persistence, they will be savvy and ready for the adult world of finance. Then by adding character-building lessons taught by Mary Kay Ash, you have given your children not only the roots to secure their futures, but also the wings to enjoy the ride.

Here's an idea: As the perfect graduation gift, hand your children this book. What better way to step into adulthood than armed with ten laws for living rich—a gift that will serve them well for a lifetime!

Your parents and money

According to a 1998 survey for the National Partnership for Women & Families, two in three Americans in their 30s expect to have responsibility for an elderly relative in their lifetime. How do you approach the topic of finances with your parents?

It's not easy. When many of us were growing up, money was a subject discussed behind closed doors. Certainly children weren't privy to financial decisions. I remember as a child wondering if we were poor or rich. I had no idea. I guess if we had been rich, it would probably have been clearer. The point is, your parents probably kept money talk to themselves. And now, it's up to you to break down that wall and talk about health care and financial issues.

*Don't be afraid to help your parents prepare
their wills, powers of attorney, health-care proxies
and other money documents.*

According to a variety of experts, here are the essentials to include in your conversation:

- The location of the following documents:
  - –their will
  - –all bank account and investment records
  - –Social Security records including Social Security numbers
  - –insurance policies
  - –pension records
  - –mortgage papers
  - –telephone numbers of their attorneys, accountants and financial advisers

It is also helpful to know if your parents have executed the following four basic estate planning documents. If any of these are more than five years old, they should be updated.

- **A will**—telling how assets are to be distributed, who will serve as executor, trustee or guardian, and how taxes will be paid from the estate (best prepared with the help of an attorney).

- **A durable power of attorney**—naming the individual who will act on a person's behalf if he or she is physically or mentally incapacitated. A living trust can serve the same purpose (best prepared with the help of an attorney).

- **A living will**—describing whether or not life-prolonging medical procedures should be used in case of serious illness or injury (may be bought in a kit from a state bar or medical association).

- **A durable power-of-attorney for health care**—naming a person to make health-care decisions for someone too ill to make his or her own decisions (can be bought from a state bar or medical association).

*Ask your parents to roll back the clock and share with you
how they handled and invested their money and how
those strategies worked for them.*

Health-care issues should also be covered. Although Medicare Parts A and B will probably cover a large portion of their medical needs, Medicare doesn't cover everything. You may wish to suggest that your parents secure a Medigap policy or a Medicare HMO to cover the gaps in traditional Medicare benefits. You may also want to consider helping them find and purchase a long-term care insurance policy (see Chapter 6 for details about long-term care insurance).

Your goal in this conversation is not to know the exact details or amounts and figures of your parents' finances if they seem reluctant to talk about these issues. Your goal is to learn how to find the information you'll need when you'll need it. To ease into the conversation you may try talking about this subject in context of your own estate planning. You may say something like, "Bob and I are working with a lawyer on our will right now, and I'd like you to know his name and where to find a copy of our will. . . ." You may connect your conversation with a recent experience such as, "Mom, how did you feel about Aunt Alma moving in with her daughter last month?" Or, "Dad, did you agree with the way Uncle Neil's family dealt with his long-term care?" Or maybe this book could be your bridge into the conversation, "I was reading a book about personal finance and estate planning and it really made me think about the questions I should have already asked you about your wishes. . . . "

This conversation is about love and respect for your parents and their wishes. Approach it that way, and it may be easier than you think. Good luck!

Six Most Important Things to Do to Team Up

1. Have a heart-to-heart conversation with your husband about money.

2. If you and your husband have polar positions on money, try role reversal for a week. Then try to move toward more middle ground in your money styles.

3. Vow to avoid the common mistakes women in couples make. (If you need a refresher, they are on page 166.)

4. Teach your children about cash flow, investing, credit cards and persistence.

5. When your children graduate from high school, give them a copy of this book.

6. Have a conversation with your parents about health care and financial issues.

Definitions of Living Rich

Freedom of choice without one moment of guilt.
—*Sabrina Johnson*

Being able to let my husband pursue his dreams and
being there for my teenager!
—*Ronnie Gribble*

Being able to help others.
—*April Howell*

Being able to treat special friends and family members to
vacations and having a generous retirement account.
—*Vicki Waddill*

Being able to manage expenses after I lost my husband
14 years ago. I was left with four children, a mortgage,
hospital bills and funeral expenses, but I made it!
—*Faye Telford King*

Living my dream of being all that God intended for me to be.
—*Jean Lewis*

Peace of mind.
—*Betty Lehr*

Being the me I want to be.
—*Kenna Colwell*

Living a Rich Life

CHAPTER EIGHT

Law #8: Sow Good. Receive Good

The seeds you plant in the hearts and minds of others will be what you receive in return—tenfold. Only sow that which you wish to receive in return. Sow good. Receive good. —MARY KAY ASH

THE LAW OF THE HARVEST COMES STRAIGHT FROM THE BIBLE and was chosen by Mary Kay Ash to be the foundation for her highest award—the Go-Give Award. There's a lesson of abundance here that's important in our quest to live a rich life. That lesson is this: There's no mention in this law of giving *if* and *when* we have a lot of money or that the gift we give should be made of money. The lesson implied in this law of the harvest is that we all have *enough* to be givers and the more we give, the richer we'll feel. That's the harvest—recognizing the abundance of our lives as we stand today and feeling the rich rewards that come from sharing that abundance with others.

I don't want to belabor this point, but it's so beautiful and so critical in living a rich life—indulge me as we dig a little deeper into this thought. Some people may think that it's easy for rich people to give. That's why they do it. Think again. Remember three things: 1) it's not all about *money*, 2) we all have *enough* and 3) it's only *after* we give that we truly feel rich, not before.

Think about it—you have more understanding than some people, don't you? Give it away. You have more compassion than some, don't you? Give it away. You have more tolerance than some, don't you? Give it away. You absolutely have to think in terms of what you have rather than what you don't have if you want to live rich. When you focus on what you have rather than what you don't have, you live from abundance. And when you live from abundance, you will always find a gift you can give exactly at the time it needs to be given. And the harvest? You'll feel rich. You'll *be* rich.

It reminds me of the concept of going the second mile. Ever wonder where that saying came from? Again, there's a Biblical origin. In the time of the Roman Empire, Roman soldiers had the right to ask any subject of the empire to carry their baggage one mile—that was the limit, one mile. So, people who carried the load of the soldiers one mile were required to do so by law—they were essentially slaves for that one mile. Then Jesus came along and had a different idea—he encouraged people to carry the load a second mile. Why go beyond what they had to? Simple—when they carried those bags the second mile, they were exercising free will. They were no longer slaves; they were free men living from abundance. That second mile became a gift. They gave it and with every step of their giving, they felt more and more in control of their lives. Then when they sat those bags down at the feet of the Roman soldiers, they looked them in the eyes and, rather than feeling like slaves, they felt abundantly free. That was their harvest.

Essentially you have that same choice today. You can do the bare minimum . . . go no further than the first mile covering your obligations and harvesting a feeling of scarcity as a result. Or you can go the second mile, give some of yourself, some of your heart and possibly some of your bank account, and harvest a feeling of abundance. Your harvest. Your choice.

LESSON IN COUNTING YOUR BLESSINGS

I started my Mary Kay business in 1991. I was serving a church full-time as a Presbyterian minister. I have a Master of Divinity degree and I loved the whole principle and calling of ministry and serving God and others. When I turned 30, however, I knew my life was out of balance. I wanted to fix it and that's when Mary Kay came along. I started my Mary Kay business knowing that I had to do it, but not really knowing why. I felt called! That same year we found out that I couldn't have more children. We have a son and I wanted so much also to have a girl. I served my church for two more years. During that year I was sitting at the table with my son Lance and he said something that forever changed my life. He said, "Mom, I wish I were a girl." Naturally, I asked him why and he said, "Because, Mom, then you would be happy." That was my wake-up call. That day I knew I had to start appreciating the blessings I had. Since that day I've given thanks for Lance every single day. I started looking at what I did have instead of what I didn't. From that day forward, I invested in other people. As a result, I've been given blessings beyond my imagination. The ultimate of those blessings is a little girl brought to me through a Mary Kay contact. On the way home from Leadership Conference in 1999, my husband called and said he wanted to meet me halfway. When we met, he handed me his phone and asked me to call for my messages. There was a message from a Consultant who had been in my unit for a short time. She said she had met someone looking for an adoptive family and asked if we would be interested. I believe if we celebrate what we do have, give ourselves to others so they have the same perspective, blessings will come. It's been an amazing year. Our daughter was born on April 7, 1999. We were all there for her birth. The adoption was final on October 20. I was able to cover all the substantial costs involved with my savings from my Mary Kay business. We paid cash for everything. I am so grateful my daughter came via Mary Kay. She is a living symbol of Mary Kay's dream; this blessing happened because of what Mary Kay sowed in so many people's lives and the investment she made through this Company in me.

—RENEE HACKLEMAN, Independent Senior Sales Director

Real life sowing and reaping

If someone asks for something, and if you respect the law of the harvest, your response must be to give something. This doesn't necessarily mean you will give exactly what's requested, but simply that you should give of something you possess in plenty. Maybe a word of encouragement? Maybe a tip you found profitable in business? Maybe extra time in conversation with a friend? Maybe a smile to a stranger on the street? Maybe the go-ahead to a frustrated driver weaving into traffic? What do you have in abundance? Courtesy? Time? Compassion? Wisdom? Think of what you possess in plenty and give it every chance you get. It makes great abundance training!

Here's a perfect example. A story appeared on my e-mail on the precise day I was writing this particular section of this chapter. In the e-mail I was asked to pass the story along to a friend . . . so here it is, my friend, a wonderful lesson about giving:

> He almost didn't see the old lady, stranded on the side of the road. But even in the dim light of day, he could see she needed help. So he pulled up in front of her Mercedes and got out. His old car was still sputtering when he approached her. Even with the smile on his face, she was worried. No one had stopped to help for the last hour or so. Was he going to hurt her? He didn't look safe—he looked poor and hungry. He could see that she was frightened, standing out there in the cold, so he said, "I'm here to help you, ma'am. Why don't you wait in the car where it's warm? By the way, my name is Brian."
>
> Brian crawled under the car looking for a place to put the jack. After skinning his knuckles a time or two and adding dirt to his pants and shirt, Brian began tightening up the lug nuts. As he did, the old lady rolled down the window and told him she couldn't thank him enough and asked how much she owed him.

Brian just smiled as he closed her trunk. He had never thought about money. This was not a job to him. This was helping someone in need. He had lived his whole life that way. He told her that if she really wanted to pay him back, the next time she saw someone who needed help, she could give it and think of him when she did.

A few miles down the road the lady saw a small café. She went in to grab a bite to eat and take the chill off before she made the last leg of her trip home. It was a dingy-looking restaurant so unfamiliar to her. Her waitress came over and had such a sweet smile, one that being on her feet all day couldn't erase. The lady noticed the waitress was nearly eight months pregnant, but she never let the strain and aches change her attitude. The lady wondered how someone who had so little could be so giving. Then she remembered Brian. After the lady finished her meal and the waitress went to get change for her hundred-dollar bill, the lady slipped out the door and left. Then the waitress noticed something written on the napkin, under which she found four more hundred-dollar bills.

With tears in her eyes, she picked up the note and read, "You don't owe me anything. Somebody nice helped me out the way I'm helping you. If you really want to pay me back, here's what you do—do not let this chain of love end with you."

That night when the waitress climbed into bed, she was thinking of the money and what the lady had written. She knew how worried her husband was, so she gave him a soft kiss and whispered soft and low, "Everything's going to be all right. I love you, Brian."

Mary Kay would have summed up this story by saying, "What you send into the lives of others comes back into your own." The law of the harvest. So what does this law mean for you? How does it work in real life? Here are a few "sowing" possibilities:

- **Give of your time and your heart.** Get involved with community affairs or volunteer work. Look for opportunities to help one-on-one. Look for areas in which you feel special empathy for those you're helping. Find a supportive organization so you feel part of a team effort for change. Find a service that could use a special skill you possess. To help with your search, go online and search "volunteer opportunities." You'll be flooded with possibilities. Or call your local Chamber of Commerce for local initiatives that could benefit from your gifts.

- **Give money.** Here's the idea—by giving money, no matter how small the amount you give, you are creating a flow of cash that will return to you in some manner at some time. Financial consultants who deal with the subject of giving are consistent on this point. In fact, one went as far as to say that when you give money to others you "kick the door open" for money to return to you. Just do it and experience how you feel. When you feel that tingly sensation under your skin and the quickening of your heartbeat, you will feel the joy of giving—and that's when financial experts say you will hold the key to unlimited wealth.

*According to Dr. Redford Williams,
director of behavioral research at Duke University,
research studies have found that people who volunteered
had greater longevity and reported better health
than their nonvolunteer counterparts.*

All sound a bit crazy? Let's take the concept out of the clouds and put it in more logical terms. The more you're able to feel great about giving cash to others, the more you can shift into thinking that others will feel great about giving cash to you. We touched on this mind-shift in Chapter 6 when we talked about disconnecting spending money with pain and connecting it instead to joy. The giving concept requires the same mind-shift. If you feel the sweet and deep joy of giving from the heart without expectation of any exchange, financial consultants say you are ready to receive extra cash into your life.

I recently had the opportunity to feel the joy of giving, even though it grew out of sadness. A close friend of mine died who was the epitome of a giving heart. In his honor, I pulled out 20 envelopes and addressed them to a random group of people in my address book. I placed in each envelope a $5 bill along with this paragraph:

> I'm sending this in remembrance and honor of a friend who lost to cancer but won in life. He taught me by example that giving is a blessing. He gave to people with only one stipulation—that they give to others in return. Use this gift however you like, and when someone you meet needs something from you, give it with an open heart and in loving remembrance of a man who taught us well.

Of course, I sent these envelopes with no signature and no return address. There was nothing to be expected in return but the knowledge that someone would open the envelope and feel warm and committed to giving. My "harvest" was the wonderful feeling that I could extend the reach of my friend just a little bit further. You may want to try something similar. Mail plain anonymous envelopes with $1 or $2 bills (you can get them at any bank) and a short note of kindness to a random group of people. This could be the very exercise you need to invite abundance into your bank account. At the very least, you'll invite joy into your heart. Try it and see for yourself.

Of course, we all have before us another opportunity to make a difference for others through our donations of cash to the Mary Kay Ash Charitable Foundation. Follow the work of this foundation and don't miss the joy of being a part of this team effort to help women and families in need.

- **Remember, giving may be a part of your estate plan.** We talked about leaving a legacy in Chapter 5 and how to plan for the property side of that legacy through estate planning. The emphasis here is the benefit you'll receive from the "giving" strategies of estate planning. For example, by setting up a charitable trust along with a wealth replacement trust outlined on page 115, you can claim a charitable deduction on your income taxes during your lifetime (possibly saving you in taxes the amount you need to pay the life insurance premium to replace your estate for your heirs), and you're able to give a substantial contribution to a charity close to your heart. Check with a tax attorney or estate planner to see if this form of giving is appropriate for you.

The typical family throws away hundreds of dollars of things every year that could be fixed up and used. Why not give these items to the Salvation Army or other charitable organizations? You can deduct the fair market value of your donation from your taxes. For the 15 minutes it will take you to list the contributions and get a receipt, you may be able to save in taxes.

*In a 1994 survey of working women
by the U.S. Department of Labor, more than half
of the respondents cited as priorities for change
on-the-job training and having more responsibility
for how they do their jobs—a gift of change
you can provide.*

- **Give to women the gift of Mary Kay.** You have one other gift in your possession that will begin the flow of wealth back to you. That gift is the gift of Mary Kay. I asked Sales Directors through the *Mary Kay InTouch®* program to describe to me the Mary Kay opportunity as if it were packaged in a gift box. If you opened that box, what would you see? Here are two responses. They are both poetic. Search through the imagery and find the true gifts they describe:

> "If the Mary Kay opportunity were in a gift box, the box would be overflowing with rainbows, sunshine and glittery stars. I would feel warmth and love when I opened it."
>
> —*Leanne Sexton*, Independent Senior Sales Director

> "In the gift box of Mary Kay, I would see a vast ocean with wonderful waves. I would feel sun like honey. I would smell the certainty of life everlasting. I would use the perspective of forever when I shook out the tissue and let it flutter in the breeze."
>
> —*Anne Johns*, Independent Senior Sales Director

Do you see the true gifts in those two gift boxes? The gifts of possibility, of peace, of recognition, of support, of love, of becoming, of sweet friendship, of time-honored principles, of freedom. Those are the gifts you have to offer. The message is simple—treat your business as a gift. Give it with love and concern for women—not out of expectation for return, but for the sweet and deep joy of giving. You don't have to force the law of the harvest. It's inevitable.

LESSON IN SISTERHOOD

Two years ago, my 19-year-old college student, Benjamin, decided to travel to another state to work for a construction company on his summer break. The construction company had made living arrangements, but as it turned out, these arrangements were hardly livable. Ben called the night he arrived and said, "Mom, I'm here, but I can't stay where they've put me." My mind started racing. How bad could it be? I asked him if he could sleep in the bathtub for just one night and his response was, "No, Mom, even the bathtub is brown!" That's when I asked him to get a phone book and look in the Yellow Pages for Mary Kay Cosmetics. He thought I had lost my mind asking him to check out the business at a time like this. But he did, and the next morning I was on the phone to a Mary Kay Independent Sales Director who I had never met asking her to help my son. Her name was Debra Barnett, and even though we didn't know one another personally, she took the time to find my son a place to rent for the summer and treated him as if she had known him all his life! Being able to count on each other just as you would a sister—that's *what makes life in Mary Kay so rich!*

— **BELVA FRITZ, Independent Sales Director**

REAL TRUE THOUGHTS GO TO HAPPY GIVERS

This line comes from a poem written in 1998 by a 12-year-old boy named Marshall Ball who was born with a host of difficulties, including the inability to speak. Marshall communicates by pointing to specific letters on an alphabet board, which are then transcribed by family members. His phrasing is unexpected, but in his words you hear the purity of his spirit and the love in his heart. His poetry is simple but profound and ideal to complete this chapter. This poem comes from his book, *Kiss of God, The Wisdom of a Silent Child:*[1]

Choices Are Yours

The now I give
to a good thinker.

Go to feelings
that give good
to others.

You make the choice
to think
good or bad.

Real true thoughts
go to happy givers.

Begin now
to make good choices.

⌒

In It's a Wonderful Life, *Jimmy Stewart's*
character operated Bailey Savings and Loan.
He helped people at every opportunity, totally selflessly.
Then what happened when he needed help?
The gifts he gave came flooding back to him.
Sure it was just a movie. Life doesn't really work
that way for everyone—but it can for you.
Find out for yourself. Give, give, give and
produce your own wonderful life!

⌒

Six Most Important Things to Do to Sow Good and Receive Good

1. Begin now to make good choices—give something you possess in plenty to someone within the next 30 minutes.

2. The next time someone asks for something, give something. Compassion? Time? Courtesy? Respect? It's your choice.

3. Find a volunteer opportunity and give a portion of yourself. Take your children along with you on a "giving" experience.

4. Give cash anonymously to others. The amount doesn't matter—the feeling of giving without expecting does.

5. Review your estate plan for opportunities to include giving strategies.

6. Offer the gift of the Mary Kay opportunity to women you care about.

Definitions of Living Rich

Making personal choices based on faith, family and career.
—*Celia Helms*

Having quality of life, a happy heart and freedom of choice.
—*Ruthie Bresette*

Having the means to touch lives in many ways.
—*Teresa Hockett*

Enriching the lives of others.
—*Carol Borges*

Being able to be an independent, professional businesswoman
and also a mom who gets her children on the school bus
and volunteers as a room mother. God first, family second,
career third.
—*Julie Olszewski*

Not having to live paycheck to paycheck.
—*Judy O'Reilly*

Being surrounded by real people who care about me.
—*Renie Jordan*

Being able to give gifts to friends whenever I feel like it
without worrying about the cost.
—*Gloria Leek*

Living a Rich Life

CHAPTER NINE

Law #9: Turn Stumbling Blocks into Stepping Stones

Don't let the negatives of life control you. Rise above them. Use them as your stepping stones to go higher than you ever dreamed possible. We can't always control the events of our lives, but we can control our reactions to those events. — MARY KAY ASH

A TON—LITERALLY A TON—of Arkansas river rock was delivered to my backyard last week. It took nature thousands of years to grind those stones smooth along the river's bottom. And now they've become stepping stones around my flower beds. Adversity is like that rushing river water—it knocks off the rough edges in our lives—a little here and a little there. We can't control adversity, as Mary Kay said. We can, however, control our reaction to it. And it's our *reaction*—the courage to face it, the knowledge to understand it, the persistence to overcome it, and the openness to go beyond it—that allows the tossing and turning in the grind of life to smooth out the edges of stumbling blocks and turn them into stepping stones.

This chapter is about that kind of adversity—the kind that can make us stumble or lead us to growth. It's about the "D"mons many women have to face—debt, divorce and the death of a spouse. How do we face each one of these, grow from the experience and move on in our lives? Julian Sleigh, in his book *Crisis Points—Working Through Personal Problems*,[1] refers to the demons in our lives as bearers of gifts hidden under their wings. "If we challenge them and make them yield up their gifts," he says, "they will be satisfied and will fly away leaving us to benefit from what they have brought."

Now is the time to challenge those "D"mons and benefit from the lessons we learn in the process. "If we had no winter, the spring would not be so pleasant," wrote Anne Bradstreet in *Meditations Divine and Moral*. So let's explore winter for a while and use the knowledge we gain as stepping stones into spring.

Debt

We'll begin with debt. A host of books and magazine articles have been written of late as to the avalanche of debt that has consumed the American family. Binge-charging has become society's latest bugaboo—a plague of MasterCarditis and Visarhea of epidemic proportions. Maybe you've experienced the symptoms of these diseases—a wave of nausea and light-headedness when you open your credit-card statements. Or maybe you've suffered from AmEx-nesia—forgetting how much you've charged on

The Consumer Federation of America estimated 60 percent of American consumers revolve balances each month and spend an average of $1,000 per year on fees and interest—more than they pay on electricity, telephone service, car repairs or insurance.

your American Express but breaking into a sweat just thinking about seeing the balance next month. These diseases not only seem to be chronic—they also seem to be contagious since half of all U.S. households now carry $7,000 in credit-card debt.

How did it all begin? How do you make it end?

Well, we can thank Mr. Isaac Singer for the beginning. History tells us the first installment debt came in 1856, when Isaac Singer let customers take home his $125 sewing machine without full payment. Instead, they promised to pay a set amount monthly. That's when affordability no longer meant if you had money in your pocket to pay for the item outright. The question became if you had money to pay the monthly payments. Then in 1951, this shift in measuring affordability became universal. The Franklin National Bank of Long Island issued the first plastic card that let cardholders purchase anything their hearts desired without using cash or checks. The plastic revolution began.

Instead of sitting on short-term savings, use that money to pay off credit-card balances. Why would you invest in a 5-percent certificate of deposit when you have a loan costing you 16 percent?

Charging through life in the grips of a plastic card became accepted in the '60s and '70s and downright prestigious in the '80s. Then the spree turned ugly. Recriminations and guilt rode in with the '90s. The fog lifted. The party ended. And by the end of the decade, it became painfully clear that committing tomorrow's dollars for today's goodies was an unhealthy choice for mind, body, soul and pocketbook.

So what now? How is your credit health? Is it less than the best and you suffer from occasional bouts of MasterCarditis, Visarhea or AmEx-nesia? How do you make it stop?

The first step is the examination. *Then* the cure.

THE EXAMINATION

Here's the consensus of most financial consultants—if you're shelling out 20 percent or more of total after-tax income to pay your nonmortgage debts each month, you're headed for trouble. Most experts say that, depending upon your specific age and situation, monthly debt payments for everything except your mortgage should not go over 10 percent to 15 percent of your take-home pay. The financial term for this percentage is "debt-to-income ratio." Mortgage debt is not considered in this ratio since it's backed by an appreciating asset that eventually adds to your net worth. However, if you want to add it in and look at the whole package, experts say your monthly debt payments, including your mortgage, should not go over 40 percent of your pretax income.

To help you calculate your specific debt-to-income ratio, fill out this worksheet adapted from *The Money Book of Personal Finance* by Richard Eisenberg,[2] published by Warner Books:

Loans and Charge Accounts: Last month's payment:
(do not list first mortgages or credit cards you pay off each month)

_____	$_____
_____	$_____
_____	$_____
_____	$_____
_____	$_____
_____	$_____
_____	$_____
_____	$_____
_____	$_____
_____	$_____

1. Last month's total payments: $_____
2. Monthly after-tax income: $_____

3. To get your debt-to-income ratio, divide line 1 by line 2. This is the percentage of your take-home pay that goes to pay your nonmortgage debt _____%

4. Find yourself in the table below to determine your credit health:

If your age is:	and line 3 is:			
	0 to 10%	10% to 15%	15% to 20%	20%
35 to 55 *(one wage earner in household)*	Fine	Caution	Danger	Danger
35 to 55 *(two wage earners)*	Fine	Fine	Caution	Danger
Over 55	Fine	Caution	Danger	Danger

Even if you fall within the "Fine" or "Caution" category, the Consumer Credit Counseling Services organization says you may be headed for trouble if three or more of the situations below apply to you:

1. You are borrowing from one lender to pay old debts from another.

2. You hold more than ten credit cards, including gasoline company and department store cards.

3. You're unable to save at least 10 percent of your gross income because of your debt payments.

4. You only make the minimum payments listed on your credit cards.

5. You've had to ask a friend or relative to cosign a loan for you because your credit record has been damaged.

6. You have no idea how much money you actually owe.

7. You are using savings for daily expenses.

8. You are using cash advances from credit-card issuers to pay daily expenses.

9. You miss some payments and pay late on others.

10. You and your husband argue a lot about money problems or, even worse, you avoid discussing finances altogether.

CLOSER EXAMINATION

While you're examining your credit health, it's a great idea to get a copy of your current credit report from the three largest credit bureaus in the country. Experts suggest you go through this process once a year to be sure the information on your report is accurate. You will need to submit a written request for your report. Fees vary depending on the bureau, your state of residence and your specific situation. Call for details before submitting your request.

Equifax Credit Information Services
P.O. Box 105873
Atlanta, GA 30348
1-800-685-1111
www.equifax.com/consumer/consumer.html

Trans Union LLC
212 S. Market
Wichita, KS 67202
1-800-888-4213
www.tuc.com

Experian (formerly TRW)
P.O. Box 2104
Allen, TX 75013-2104
1-888-397-3742
www.experian.com

THE CURE

If you have credit-card debt, financial experts recommend you pay off this debt before you plan any other investments. Here are the steps to take:

1. List your debts in order from the highest to lowest interest rates. For example:

Creditor	Amount due	Interest rate
XYZ Visa	$2,318	18%
Discover	$3,199	15%
Car loan	$6,550	9%
Student loan	$3,200	5%

2. Next, set your payoff priorities. Again, focus on the loans with the highest interest rates first.

   Or you may want to try a method suggested by financial consultant Henry S. Brock. Here is the gist of his idea: Rank your monthly payments by dollar amount from the largest dollar amount down to the smallest. Double your payment on the smallest payment. When that debt is paid, add the doubled payment plus the minimum payment on the next debt up the list. When that next debt is paid, apply the first doubled payment plus the minimum payment for the second debt and apply it to the next one up. Even if you're in severe debt, it may take four to five years, but you can clear your debts if you stop borrowing and stick with this plan.

3. If you're overwhelmed by this process and feel you need help, there are solutions out there. You may want to contact a non-profit credit management service. These agencies can help you set up a budget, trim your expenses, negotiate with your creditors to reduce interest rates and develop repayment plans.

Here are a few of your choices given for your convenience only. Mary Kay Inc. does not endorse any specific counseling organization.

- **Consumer Credit Counseling Service,**
  1-800-388-2227, www.nfcc.org

  Consumer Credit Counseling Service is a member of the National Foundation for Consumer Credit, the nation's oldest and largest network of nonprofit credit counseling organizations. When you call the toll-free number, you will be transferred to the office nearest you. You can then make an appointment, gather together your bills and talk to a certified counselor in a confidential session.

- **Genus Credit Management,** 1-800-955-0412, www.genus.org
  The initial interview and all interaction that occurs afterward is handled over the phone or through e-mail.

- **Money Management International,** 1-800-762-2271,
  www.mmintl.org/
  This service offers counseling over the telephone, by e-mail, fax and traditional mail.

- **Debt Counselors of America®,** 1-800-680-DEBT (3328),
  www.dca.org/
  Lots of free information and publications are available on this Web site. This nonprofit organization helps consumers get out of debt without bankruptcy or consolidation loans.

- **Debtors Anonymous,** 212-969-8111, www.danyc.org
  This organization offers local support groups all over the country. When you call its hotline listed here, you will hear a recording of the organization's purpose.

LESSON IN OVERCOMING DEBT

I started my Mary Kay business to make an extra $500 a month to help get out of debt. I had credit-card debt of $35,000. I had about 12 to 15 cards, but my husband thought we only had one. I took one card up to $10,000 three months after I got it. Within eight months after starting my Mary Kay business, I was able to get out of debt except for one card—the big one carrying $10,000. That one took me three years. Then I did the same thing again—got into debt of about $35,000 and had to dig my way out again. Now we are debt-free with the exception of our house. The lessons I learned during all this were many. I learned to be open and honest with everyone about debt. I learned to tell people what the signs are when I'm making bad decisions so they can point them out to me when necessary. This helps open the lines of communication even more. I learned that I don't want a credit card. I only use a debit card and an American Express. I learned not to count on a big month to pay off big debts. I learned to put money back for the low months so I don't get behind again. I learned to talk all the time with my unit about being debt-free. I share with them a formula that worked for me. The formula goes like this: You make four columns on a sheet of paper. In the first column you list your credit cards. In the second column place the balances. In the third column place the minimum payments. In the fourth write down what you're paying. Pick out the card with the lowest balance and focus on paying that one off. Then take the money you paid on that one plus the minimum payment for the next card and apply it to the next highest balance. At the same time build a reserve in a money-market account so you don't get in trouble again. This is not a quick fix, but it worked for me.

—**DIANA SUMPTER**, **Independent Executive Senior Sales Director**

THE RECOVERY

So far we've talked in terms of dollars owed, payback amounts and years of payment—all numbers we can manage and control. Debt recovery, the kind that permanently gets you off the roller coaster of chronic debting, is another matter—a matter of attitude toward living. If debt is a problem and always has been in your life, listen up to financial consultant Colette Dowling. She says debt recovery requires a change not only in your spending habits, but in you. In her article, "Real Recovery" at iVillage.com, Ms. Dowling says that to live a rich life and enjoy a feeling of abundance, you must understand that:

- "No one owes you anything.

- "You and no one else is responsible for *you*.

- "Getting your bills paid on time deserves acknowledgment from you but not praise. You don't get kudos for acting like an adult. . . .

- "Blaming others is self-destructive. [It's not about anyone but you.]

- "Debting results from a negative rather than a positive attitude toward life. It comes from feeling deprived or from feeling unrealistically entitled."[3]

In other words, to make a difference in debt, you must make a change in you. A friend once sent me this autobiography by an unknown author that describes this process of adversity, discovery and change. In which chapter are you?

Chapter 1:
I walk down the street. There is a deep hole in the
sidewalk. I fall in. I am helpless. It isn't my fault.
It takes forever to find a way out.

Chapter 2:

I walk down the same street. There is a deep hole in the sidewalk. I pretend I don't see it. I fall in again. I can't believe I'm in the same place. But it isn't my fault. It still takes a long time to get out.

Chapter 3:

I walk down the same street. There is a deep hole in the sidewalk. I see it is there. I still fall in. It's a habit, but my eyes are open. I know where I am. It is my fault. I get out immediately.

Chapter 4:

I walk down the same street. There is a deep hole in the sidewalk. I walk around it.

Chapter 5:

I walk down a different street. There are no holes.

If you've fallen into that hole of debt, find your way out and walk down a different street. Instead of worrying about holes, you'll be able to enjoy the view. Try it!

Compulsive shopping has been studied in relationship with serotonin deficiency. Serotonin is manufactured in the body from an amino acid called tryptophan. When serotonin levels fall too low, obsessive-compulsive disorders seem to appear— including, for some, compulsive shopping. For those with compulsive behaviors, the cause could be biologically determined and therefore treatable.

The advice for continued good health

Following the examination, following the cure and following recovery, it's necessary to take steps to stay healthy. Here is a collection of credit-smart advice from the experts that will help you stay debt-free and credit-healthy:

1. Don't hold credit cards with credit lines available to you that exceed 20 percent of your income.

2. Keep in mind that if you carry more than $6,000 of credit-card debt, you will pay more than $1,000 in finance charges annually (assuming an interest rate of 16 percent or more).

3. Check your credit record once a year and correct any mistakes you find.

4. Eliminate buying major items on credit by creating a category in your budget for big purchases.

5. Cancel your overdraft protection on your checking account. Some experts say the cushion allows you to lower your guard and essentially give yourself an additional way to dig into debt.

6. Remember, the gift of living rich comes to those who have interest working *for* them, not against them.

7. Dispose of all your credit-cards except one. Keep the one with the lowest interest rate and no annual fee.

8. Get a debit card from your bank and use it as you would a credit card. Establishments accept it just as they do credit cards. The difference is the fact that the funds come out of your bank account, so you're paying as you go instead of amassing debt and interest charges. Be sure to enter the purchase on your check register so you don't lose control of your balance and run into overdraft and service charges.

9. Consider setting aside an additional 5 to 10 percent of your income for reducing car loans, charge accounts, educational loans and anything else you're lugging around like a load of those Arkansas river rocks.

10. Use your credit card to go on the offensive. Charge every purchase you can on your card and take advantage of the statements as a reporting device. Some cards even give you an annual report that sorts your purchases into expense categories. Caution—this works only if you pay the balance each month. These items are a part of your budget—you're simply paying for them in one lump sum rather than with various checks.

11. Consistently hold family council meetings in which you discuss all the things your family wants. Then rank the list in order of priority and plan how to purchase these items using pay-as-you-go tactics.

12. Find "no money" ways to get what you want. Walking in the park gives your body the same benefits as walking on the treadmill at the $30-a-month gym. How about renting movies from the library? Be creative!

13. Watch out for dribble spending. Be conscious of every buying decision—remember that journal? Write down your purchases and stay focused!

14. Remember the concept of lost opportunity when applied to spending? Think about it before you make any big purchase. If you make that purchase on a credit card, the lost opportunity cost is even greater because you lose the opportunity to invest the money that covered the purchase price as well as the money needed to pay the interest charges.

15. Consumer Counseling Services advises this: When you make a credit-card purchase, enter the amount in your checkbook

register in order to have sufficient funds to cover the payment when your credit-card statement arrives. And do not put purchases on a credit card unless the amount is within your monthly spending limit for that category on your budget sheet.

16. Also according to Consumer Counseling Services, if you plan a large purchase, you should be prepared to pay off the amount in three monthly installments and no more than five.

17. Exercise discipline and stop borrowing. Living in debt saps the energy from your soul—not the condition for a living-rich way of life.

18. One expert suggests this: Keep your credit-card frozen in a container of solid ice in your freezer. That will certainly slow down impulsive spending on credit.

Divorce

Divorce is always devastating—any way you look at it. For the purpose of this chapter, we'll separate the emotional consequences from the financial ones and consider only the latter.

I know you don't expect to get divorced. Who does? But the fact remains that nearly half of all new marriages currently end in divorce. And the financial aftermath for women is excruciating. According to Neale S. Godfrey's book, *Making Change*,[4] one-quarter of all divorced women in America live at or below the poverty level. And get this—after a no-fault divorce, on average, the man's standard of living goes up 23 percent while the woman's standard of living drops by 10 percent. And contributing to this kind of financial devastation, statistics show that only 28 percent of divorced women get any kind of ongoing financial support from their ex-husbands and more than one-third of women who are awarded alimony or child support never see a cent of it. Sad, isn't it? But I promised we wouldn't deal with the emotional side of divorce, so forget feeling sad and let's just get smart.

If you're separated from your husband but not yet divorced, advisers suggest you change the signature authority on any joint accounts so that both of you must sign in order for any transaction to occur.

First lesson in divorce survival training: If you're in the beginning stages of a possible divorce, Ernst & Young[5] advises you to do this:

1. "Consult with an attorney who specializes in matrimonial law."

2. "Find out what you're worth." Determine which assets qualify as marital assets and which are nonmarital. Look at how much debt you owe together.

3. "Open your own checking account if you haven't done so already." Even if you're in the arms of sweet marital bliss, it's a good idea to have your own account.

4. "[Calculate] your current living expenses. . . ."

5. "Review your insurance." Consider these issues—will you and your children still be covered under your former husband's health insurance plan? Rework your beneficiary designations on your life insurance plans. Remember the importance of your having disability insurance.

In addition, we suggest that you find out what property distribution laws are in your state. Some states are considered equitable distribution states and others are community property states.

Life *after* divorce has its own "to do" list, suggested by financial journalist Kerry Hannon for iVillage.com.[6] Here are some of her suggestions, with our enumeration:

1. Get your divorce paperwork organized. These include "your final divorce decree and settlement papers, such as alimony and child-support agreements and any property sales you received in the settlement. Put the originals in a safe-deposit box and a copy in your divorce file at home, and be sure your lawyer has a copy as well."

2. Get a strong handle on your spending. "Go over the past year's credit-card bills and bank statements and that may be a good guide. Then divide [your expenses] into categories such as housing, entertainment, food, and so forth." Remember, this is a time for careful spending and complete responsibility for your money and your life. Indulge yourself in hot baths and other "no-money" kinds of ways and avoid the big purchases. This is a time you need to hang onto your money rather than spend it on things that give you a momentary lift.

3. "Be sure that any asset that was registered in both your names is changed, such as your car registration or brokerage accounts."

4. "Update your will, if you haven't already."

5. Inform your creditors that you are divorced. Tell them the debts your former husband is now responsible for paying.

Ask them to notify you if these debts aren't paid so that your credit rating doesn't get tarnished by mistake.

6. Review your investment portfolio with an investment adviser to be sure your investments are allocated appropriately for your new situation.

7. Record all child support payments so you will have an accurate picture of the timeliness and amounts of payments.

8. If you have custody of your children, keep good records of their expenses. If you ever need to show the real expense of raising children compared to the child support being paid, you will have the documentation necessary.

9. Be careful not to let "guilt" dictate your spending decisions regarding your children. "Spending on extras just to make your kids feel better is not the right approach." Talk with them instead, be open with them about your financial situation and simply love them. They will love you back, and you'll have more money saved toward their college education in the process.

On July 22, 1998, a law became effective that makes it easier for divorced women to prove they were innocent of any tax misrepresentations of which they were unaware. This is important to you if you filed joint tax returns with your ex-husband prior to this year.

LESSON IN LIVING SINGLE

My husband left the week I started my Mary Kay business. I had six people to support. Most of my early career was focusing on my children and making money while working my business around our normal life. In my first week, I had about $1,000 in sales, which showed me that I could make great money with my Mary Kay business and would never need to go back to my former job as a legal secretary. In my first year, my business goal was to become an Independent Sales Director and earn the use of a pink Cadillac so that I could have a brand-new car and no car payment. My second goal was to build my team to the point that I could make my mortgage payment with my personal team commission check each month. I felt if I had my mortgage payment and car payment covered, I could manage. My Sales Director commission check more than covered my household expenses and my sales gave us all the extras. In other words, I learned to "earmark" money, which gave me very real goals to accomplish. I always had a weekly goal for what I wanted, not just for what I needed. If on Wednesday I wasn't halfway there, I did more. I didn't want to live where I didn't have enough money because I knew there was plenty of money in Mary Kay. I always visualized being a top Cadillac-driving Mary Kay Million-Dollar Sales Director and used all the sources of income available with a Mary Kay business so I never felt afraid. I knew there was always a way to make more cash. I taught my children an abundance mentality because we lived it. If there was something they wanted and we didn't have the money, I would say, "Yes, the money is coming. I'll let you know when it gets here." They learned to expect that money was coming in all the time. That helped me work at a higher level. It is so exciting to be working toward my goal to be an Independent National Sales Director this year and to see other women with the freedom to have a great Mary Kay career and the satisfaction of being available to their families. We have it all!

— **KATHY LEE, Independent Executive Senior Sales Director**

Death of a spouse

Widows make up about 11 percent of the adult female population in the United States. Unfortunately, death of a spouse happens, and when it does, it can be one of the most traumatic events in your life. It will leave you feeling confused, alone and so emotionally exhausted you're numb, but that won't stop the bills from coming or your financial concerns from demanding your attention. This is the last thing you care about at this point, but it's important that you don't shut down. Take charge as best you can. Here are the composite suggestions from the experts to help you manage financial matters through the grieving process:

Before it happens

Right now, before any possibility you're left a widow, there are steps you should take to ensure your financial well-being.

- Make sure your husband has adequate life insurance so that, in the case of his death, the sum of the death benefit is sufficient to produce an investment income that will maintain your current standard of living. The general rule of thumb used by financial consultants is to purchase life insurance in the amount of five times your husband's annual income.

- Know where all documentation is stored. This includes joint tax returns, retirement account records, brokerage and bank account statements, your wills and insurance policies.

- Know the names and numbers of your financial and legal advisers.

- Have an up-to-date will.

- Review the future value of your estate and make appropriate estate planning decisions.

What to do just after

- Ask a close friend to notify family and friends.

- If your husband has left a letter of instruction, read it. It may outline his wishes for funeral services.

- Make funeral arrangements. Ask someone to help you call or visit at least two funeral homes and cemeteries to compare costs. According to the National Funeral Directors Association, on average, a traditional funeral costs approximately $4,800, with an additional $2,400 for in-ground burial. By law, mortuaries must give costs to consumers by telephone and provide price lists at their facilities.

- Find the will. Generally, if your husband has a probate estate worth more than $60,000, probate is required. Probate assets are those owned by your husband alone—assets he owned independently or retirement assets, annuities and life insurance proceeds that name his estate as the beneficiary. Probate is a court-supervised process and proves that a will is valid and that the property passes to the appropriate people. Probate is a routine process but can take months—possibly years—depending on the complexity of the will, the value of the estate and the number of beneficiaries. There are fees involved in probate generally based on the fair-market value of the assets in the estate, plus attorney fees and possibly a filing fee. Probate can be avoided entirely if your husband passes his property to beneficiaries outside the will. He can accomplish this in three ways: 1) all your husband's assets are placed in trusts, 2) all your husband's assets are held jointly by you and your husband, in which case they are transferred directly to you, and 3) the proceeds of a life insurance policy, an annuity or retirement fund names you or someone else as a beneficiary. If your husband dies without a will, the court appoints an administrator to settle the estate.

- Call your attorney if you have one. If you don't, call an attorney who specializes in trusts and estates.

- Begin keeping a financial diary. Log every conversation about the estate and any financial discussions you have. Keep your diary or notebook by the phone when you're home and in your purse when you go to any data-gathering meeting. Many widows discover later that they thought they were in control, but realize they didn't have their usual ability to remember conversations and decisions.

- If you are the executor of your husband's estate, you are responsible for settling the estate. To prepare for this process, advisers suggest you file away the financial tables from the local newspaper the day of your husband's death. If you have stock investments, this will provide you a record of the security prices at that time. Also, keep the monthly statement of any mutual fund or investment fund at that time.

What to do within the month

Your life may feel as if it's in total upheaval, but taking charge of your finances is one area you can control. You're being swamped with paperwork at this time, so get organized and give yourself space to work. Keep all the relevant documents in one place and use this place as your base of operations. Try to set aside a certain time each day that you work through the papers. Even if you do nothing more than make one phone call a day, you'll feel better. Action helps the healing—it's empowering. Here are other suggestions to help you through this time:

- Get a copy of your husband's death certificate and make about two dozen copies. (Your funeral director can get them for you.) Credit-card issuers, your husband's life insurance company, government offices such as the Social Security

Administration and your state's office for inheritance tax, and financial services providers such as your bank manager and stockbroker will all require this proof of death.

- Pay your bills. You may wish to get a close friend to help you through this process. Unfortunately, creditors don't give a grace period for grieving. Bills still have to be paid on time to avoid substantial interest charges, late fees and a damaged credit report.

- Notify the bank or financial institution and credit-card companies that your joint accounts need to be changed into your name only.

- Contact the Social Security Administration. You can file a benefits claim in person at a local office or by phone (800-772-1213) or by computer (www.ssa.gov). You can receive widow's benefits if you are age 60 or older. If you are a widow with children, you may be eligible for a widow's benefit at any age if you are caring for a child under the age of 16 or who is disabled. Unmarried children may receive survivors' benefits on your husband's record until they are age 18 (or 19 if they are attending school full-time).

- If your husband was employed at the time of his death, check with his employer and find out about his pension, medical insurance and life insurance offered through the company. The human resources department should be able to help you.

- Contact your husband's life insurance issuer. You will need a copy of his death certificate, the policy number and the face value of the policy, and a copy of his birth certificate. Life insurance proceeds are income-tax–free.

- If your husband served in the military, call or visit your local office of the Department of Veterans Affairs. You may be eligible for a pension, and in some cases, the government may pay for some funeral and burial costs. You will likely need a copy of his military discharge papers.

- If your husband is named the beneficiary on your life insurance policy, change the designation. Also review the beneficiary designation on your retirement accounts. This is a good time to reevaluate your coverage. If you still have dependents, you may need more coverage than before.

- Update your will. If you have minor children, be sure you name a guardian for them.

If you need a copy of a birth or marriage certificate, call the county clerk's office in the county where the birth or marriage took place. It'll supply a certified copy if you can't find the original. For a duplicate Social Security card, call Social Security at 1-800-772-1213.

What to do in the months that follow

- Eventually you will need to change the title and registration of any motor vehicles listed in your husband's name. You can do this by contacting the Department of Motor Vehicles.

- Don't rush into anything. This is one time when procrastination is a good thing. If you receive a lump sum from your husband's life insurance, refrain from investing it for at least six months. Put the cash in a money-market fund or a short-term Certificate of Deposit or in Treasury Bills. They offer a safe place to store this cash until you are ready to make choices with a clear mind.

- Be careful about "hot tips." This is a sad indictment of human-kind, but there are those out there who target widows and promise surefire investments during this time of vulnerability. Pass on any hot tips until you have time to do your own research.

LESSON IN LOSING A SPOUSE

It's been three years since my husband died. He was out running one day and his heart burst. He was perfectly healthy. I was so thankful for my Mary Kay business. It gave me a chance to fall into my work. I felt numb when it first happened, so I didn't have to deal with it for a while. That was a wonderful thing. It gave me such a feeling of love for every single day because I realize that life is so precious and so short. His death changed my whole perspective. I am much more help-ful with my people. Widowhood made me a top Independent Sales Director. I got busy because I realized that life is so short. If you're going to do something, do it. The lesson I learned was to never turn down an opportunity to take a percentage of your income and put it into your own retirement plan. When my husband died, his former wife sued for his retirement and received it. I tell Consultants they should always save at least 10 percent of their income. If your husband dies, you may not keep the house you're living in. You have to start planning. I'm 64 now and I don't know what I would do without my Mary Kay business. I have two degrees and don't want to work for someone else. I've learned that you have to take care of yourself—financially, emotionally and physically. You must do it for yourself.

—JOANNA HELTON, Independent Executive Senior Sales Director

Six Most Important Things to Do to Turn Stumbling Blocks Into Stepping Stones

1. Calculate your debt-to-income ratio to determine your credit health.

2. Get a current copy of your credit report from the three major credit bureaus and correct any inaccuracies.

3. Develop your plan to pay your credit-card balances. Focus on one card at a time and stick to your system. If you need help, contact a credit-management service.

4. After debt recovery, vow to never walk down that same debt-ridden street again.

5. If you've had to deal with divorce, take the emotion out of the financial considerations and follow the divorce survival tips in this chapter.

6. Hopefully, you'll never be placed in the role of widow. However, understand now the responsibilities of that role and prepare to make the financial repercussions as insignificant as possible.

Definitions of Living Rich

Doing anything I want to do.
—*Joanne Bell*

Being surrounded by the most incredibly positive, giving women
you could ever meet.
—*Linda Whitcher-Bunce*

Making a difference in other people's lives.
—*Gwen Whitelaw*

Living life to the fullest with the time to enjoy family,
friends, travel, grandchildren, skiing, golf—everything I love
with the people I love.
—*Judi White*

Being able to rock my babies regardless of the day of the week
or time of the day while having a pink car parked in my driveway.
—*Conni Fennell-Burley*

Having freedom and flexibility to run my life.
—*Chris Whitcher*

The ability to provide choices for my family while supporting
my chosen charities especially our church.
—*Carmen Weedston*

Being in control of your finances instead of your finances
controlling you.
—*Terrie Goshorn*

Living a Rich Life

CHAPTER TEN

Law #10: Begin Now

I would like to urge you to form the habit as of this moment of doing whatever it is that you have to do now. I hope you will make "TNT" your watchword, that is, "Today Not Tomorrow!"

— MARY KAY ASH

SCARLET O'HARA MAY HAVE CHARMED her way around Tara with that "tomorrow's another day" stuff, but for us, there's only one day that counts—today. Talk to the elderly and ask them if they regret more what they *did* during their lives or what they *didn't* do. Most will tell you their greatest regrets lie in the undone . . . the unsung . . . the un-won. As John Greeleaf Whittier wrote, "Of all sad words of tongue or pen, the saddest are these, 'It might have been.'" Don't let those words become yours. Instead, focus, commit, do. It's a simple cycle but if you get your head involved and *focus* on investing, get your heart involved and *commit* to investing, and get your body involved and *do* what it takes day in and day out to realize that commitment, you will win the finance game. Pure and simple. The trick is . . . you need to start *now*. The difference in *now* and later could be the difference

*To find out how long it will take to double your money
at a certain rate, divide 72 by the rate. For example, if earning
8 percent, it will take nine years to double your money.*

between a nest-egg and a goose-egg. It could be the difference between relaxing with a book on the patio of your free-and-clear home or hoping for a handout at Wednesday night Bible study. *Now* could mean everything. Take a look at the example that follows and see for yourself.

The cost of procrastination

Let's create a couple of hypothetical investors and look at the difference between now and ten years later. One woman, we'll call her Ann, begins investing $4,000 a year in her retirement account at age 36 and stops at age 55. Another woman, we'll call her Sarah, waits until she's 46 to get started investing $4,000 a year and continues contributing this amount until she's 65. Both Ann and Sarah have contributed $80,000 to their retirement accounts. Both have contributed over a 20-year time span. Both have realized a 12-percent average annual return on their money. Here's the difference—Ann's account when she retires at age 67 is worth $855,277.21. Sarah's is worth $329,751.99. The difference between now and ten years later is a whopping $525,525.22. Same dollars invested—dramatically different results. Why? Ann chose "now" to begin. Sarah chose ten years later.

Maybe you're not 36 anymore. That's OK. Don't throw your hands up in defeat. The point here is that no matter how many candles are on your birthday cake, *now* will create more dollars for you than *later* will. So love yourself—focus on investing, commit to investing and begin doing what it takes *now*.

COST OF PROCRASTINATION

JOAN	ELAINE	ANN	SARAH
$2,024,313.50	$1,071,826.58	$855,277.21	$329,751.99
AT AGE 67	AT AGE 67	AT AGE 65	AT AGE 65

Age	Joan	Elaine	Ann	Sarah
66–61 / AGE 60	$0 INVESTED	$2,000 INVESTED EACH YR. FOR 36 YRS.	$0 INVESTED	$4,000 INVESTED EACH YR. FOR 20 YRS.
59–51 / AGE 50			$4,000 INVESTED EACH YR. FOR 19 YRS.	
49–41 / AGE 40				$0 INVESTED
39–31 / AGE 30	$2,000 INVESTED EACH YR. FOR 10 YRS.	$0 INVESTED	$0 INVESTED	
29–20 / AGE 20				

If you need further convincing of the wisdom of the "now" strategy, take a look at this scenario on page 221: One investor, Joan, begins investing $2,000 a year at age 22 and continues through her 32nd birthday—ten years of investing $2,000 for a total investment of $20,000. Joan sits on this investment, letting compounding work its magic at a 12-percent interest rate. At age 67, Joan's $20,000 has turned into over $2 million.

Her sister, Elaine, on the other hand, started at the age Joan stopped and began investing $2,000 a year when she was 32. She kept this up all the way through her 67th birthday, making her total investment $70,000 over a period of 35 years. Elaine then began her retirement years with $1,071,826.58 in her account—$952,487.05 less than her sister even though she invested 25 years longer and $52,000 more. *Now* is profitable.

Pick-pocketing mind tricks

So if the "now" strategy makes so much sense, why don't more people jump on the investment wagon as soon as they take home their first paycheck? Well, the mind is a powerful thing—it can work for us and it can work against us. You have to focus and commit before you can do, and it's in those first two steps that humankind tends to get bogged down.

The experts have their explanations for the mindtraps that snare us—the behavioral economists even have names for them. These explanations and tendencies have to a large degree grown from the works of economists and psychologists Richard Thaler, Daniel Kahneman and Amos Tversky. The translation of these works in terms the rest of us can understand was done by Gary Belsky and Thomas Gilovich in their book, *Why Smart People Make Big Money Mistakes*,[1] which was the source for all of the examples in the next eight pages. Essentially, the research and conclusions of these accomplished experts speak straight to the point

LESSON ABOUT LIVING IN THE DIN DIN CLUB

ndependent National Sales Director Arlene Lenarz had what she called the DIN DIN Club—Do It Now, Do It Now. So I learned from her that if an idea comes, do it now. I don't put off anything. Years ago, my husband Ken had a little aluminum boat. He would be out on the water and would be almost drowned by the waves of the big boats that sailed by. As he was sitting there soaked, he would also look up and see the condominiums on the shore and think about how great it would be to have a lake house and a decent-sized boat. He told me about that dream and I loved the idea. So, I saved all my personal team commissions for three years and put a downpayment on a house on the lake. Then we had a grandchild, and I thought it would be nice to have a pontoon boat for the grandchildren so I saved all my personal team commissions again (about $1000 a month). A year later I bought the pontoon boat with cash. I saved for three more years and paid cash for a new bass boat for my husband. Being able to get what we wanted was not always possible. One year before I started my Mary Kay business, we had very little and our daughter got a pencil sharpener for Christmas. Not too long ago I took my whole family to Hawaii for Christmas. Besides believing in "doing it now," I also believe in positive affirmations. I tell Consultants to write where they want to be on 3" by 5" cards and place these cards by the phone, on the mirror, on the dashboard in the car. I also help them record their positive affirmations on a tape and encourage them to listen to the tape in the car. It's powerful to hear your own voice. So the lessons I'd like to pass along to others are twofold: Do it now and . . . reaffirm your goals to yourself in every way possible every day. You'll get what you want!

—ASENATH BROCK, Independent National Sales Director

of why more folks don't begin *now* and act *promptly* regarding financial decisions. People suffer from decision paralysis—the biggest pick-pocket of financial futures—because of a few common thinking fallacies. Have you fallen prey to any of these mindtraps?

TOO MANY CHOICES

1. **Research shows that the more choices you have, the more likely you'll defer the decision.** Here's an illustration of this mindtrap in action as reported by Belsky and Gilovich in *Why Smart People Make Big Money Mistakes:* Psychologists Sheena Sehti and Mark Lepper conducted a study at a grocery store in Menlo Park, California. They set up two tasting booths in the store, rotating the goods every hour. During one hour the taste selection was made of 24 different jams. During the next hour the selection was scaled-down to just six jams. All tasters who approached the booth were given a $1 coupon for any jam in the store. The bar codes on the coupons identified the customers as to which selection they viewed—the 24-jam selection or the 6-jam selection. More people visited the booth when there was a greater selection of jams; however, when it came down to making a decision, only 3 percent of those exposed to the selection of 24 jams made a purchase, as opposed to 30 percent of those exposed to the set of six jams.

   What does this have to do with finances? Too much, it seems. Decision paralysis may be the reason Americans have parked $1.2 trillion in passbook savings accounts or the reason so many investors make the most conservative

If you need help crunching the numbers in preparation for investing, go to a Web site such as MoneyAdvisor (www.moneyadvisor.com) or FinanCenter (www.financenter.com) or Invesco (www.invesco.com). These sites offer retirement calculators.

investment available in their 401(k) plans with the intention of someday getting around to filtering through the choices and making a decision. Unfortunately, many times decisions never come because...

Waiting too long

2. **Research shows that the longer you wait to decide, the less likely you'll act at all.** Direct-response specialists know their biggest obstacle in a mail campaign is not their competitors, but procrastination. If that envelope gets laid down with a "tomorrow's another day" attitude, chances are excellent it won't get picked up again . . . until the day it's tossed in the trash. Psychologists Amos Tversky and Eldar Shafir illustrated this point with their own direct-response campaign presented in the Belsky and Gilovich book. The psychologists presented to university students a $5 reward for responding to a survey questionnaire. One group was given five days to respond and be awarded their $5, another group was given 21 days and the third group of students was given no deadline at all. The response went down as the days allowed went up. Sixty-six percent of the first group given the five-day deadline turned in the survey and collected the reward. Forty percent of the second group with the 21-day deadline turned in the survey and only 25 percent of the group with no deadline responded. A full 75 percent in that third group were stopped in their tracks because they just never got

> *If you're over 40 years old, a one-year delay in saving $50 a week could cost you over $18,000 in retirement.*

around to acting. You've seen the cost of this kind of delay in the calculations at the beginning of this chapter. Don't let this trap snare you.

Status-quo bias

3. **Research shows that if a decision involves change from a known to an unknown, the more likely you'll stick with the known even if it's clearly not in your best interest to do so.** Behavioral psychologists call this tendency to favor the known and comfortable the "status-quo bias." And again, a study presented in Belsky and Gilovich's book provides the perfect example of this tendency working its way into our decisions. William Samuelson of Boston University and Richard Zeckhauser of Harvard University created an experiment giving students familiar with economics and finance a problem to solve. They were told to pick one of four investment options:

Option 1: "Shares of . . . stock with a moderate risk with a 50 percent chance that over the next year its price would increase by 30 percent, a 20 percent chance it would stay the same and a 30 percent chance it would decline by 20 percent."

Option 2: "Shares of . . . stock a [bit riskier] with a 40 percent chance over the next year the price would double, a 30 percent chance it would stay the same, and a 30 percent chance it would decline by 40 percent."

Option 3: "U.S. Treasury bills with an almost certain return of 9 percent over the next year."

Option 4: "Municipal bonds with an almost certain return over the next year of 6 percent, tax-free."

As you may expect, the students given these options made their selections based on their tolerance for risk. Nothing surprising or interesting about that. The next study, however, made things more interesting. In that study the students were told they already owned one of the options and were asked to choose if they wanted to stay where they were or to switch to another option. No matter which investment choice was presented as the investment already owned, it was that known quantity that was the favorite choice every time. In the first study when all things were equal without a status-quo bias, only three in ten students chose the municipal bonds as the investment of choice. When, however, these bonds were presented as already owned by the students, nearly half of them decided the municipal bonds were the smart choice.

A 50-year-old would have to invest approximately seven times the amount a 35-year-old would have to invest to accomplish the same results.

Endorsement effect

Adding to this tendency to stick with the known, rather than making a change, is the fact that we all tend to overvalue what we own relative to the value we place on the same item owned by someone else. Belsky and Gilovich call this tendency the "endowment effect." That's why manufacturers have trial periods hoping you'll feel an ownership and therefore place a higher value on the item before decision time to buy it. It's also why some people value their current paycheck over the dollars they could have later if it were invested. That's why financial consultants suggest you place "found" money in an account for at least six months before making a decision about it. If you feel you "own" it, you will value it more and are less likely to blow it for a momentary high.

Regret aversion

4. **Research shows that if there's a possibility of a loss as a result of your decision, you're more likely to avoid that loss by avoiding that option altogether, even if the possibility of gain from that choice is greater than with any other option.** It hurts to lose, right? In fact, behavioral psychologists say we feel more strongly about the pain that comes with loss than we do about the pleasure that comes with an equal gain. Belsky and Gilovich refer to this feeling as "regret aversion." In a 1980 paper published in the *Journal of Economic Behavior and Organization*, Richard Thaler gave a hypothetical situation to illustrate this tendency, which Belsky and Gilovich presented in their book. Here is Mr. Thaler's hypothetical situation:

> *"Mr. A is in line at the movie theater. At the window as he gets his ticket, he's told he is the 100,000th customer [and as such] wins $100.*
>
> *"Mr. B is in line at different theater. The man in line in front of him is told he is the millionth customer and is awarded $1,000. [For being next in line], Mr. B wins $150."*

Which would you rather be?

Mr. Thaler writes that most people would prefer Mr. A's position, winning the $100, to that of Mr. B, who won $150. Regret aversion is at work here. Most people would feel so upset about missing out on the $1,000 award that they would prefer giving up the extra $50 to avoid the pain of loss for being one-man too late in line. How does this translate financially? Leaving cash in a savings account at the bank rather than moving it to an investment with a higher return, keeping credit-card balances on a high-rate card rather than switching that balance to a card with lower finance charges, staying in a low-paying job rather than making a commitment to your business—these are all real-life enactments of regret aversion, status-quo bias and endowment effect all rolled into one. The bottom line is decision paralysis and a substantial loss of opportunity for gain.

LESSON ABOUT THINKING IN THE NOW

When my husband's company went out of business, we thought we had two months of paychecks coming from his work. At that point I knew I had to raise my income by $4,000 a month to meet the bills of the house and keep both our children in college. My son was in an expensive school costing about $40,000 a year. When I thought of having to raise my income $4000 a month, I was paralyzed with fear. So this is what I did—I focused on a bite rather than the whole thing. I thought about what I could do at this moment toward this goal. I broke it down in the areas of income and what I could do in each area to have an immediate effect on my income. Instead of $4,000 a month, I raised my income by $5,000 a month. It was a good thing too, because as it turned out we only had one month's paycheck coming from my husband's company instead of two. That was my first lesson—allowing myself to feel the fear of a big goal, then breaking it down into the "now" by asking myself what I can do at this moment toward that goal. The next lesson I learned was to focus on people and their needs rather than my own monetary goals—to take myself entirely out of the picture as to my monetary goals so I'm focused on a higher purpose. I ask, "Why was she sent to me? What does she really want from this business?" When I think that way, I can come from a position of strength in helping her realize the benefit that fulfills her purpose. Those two approaches worked for me. Both my children graduated from college. We didn't have to sell our home, as many of our friends did who found themselves in the same position. So, if you have a big goal, give yourself the right to feel the fear, then ask what you can do right this moment. Then just do it . . . and do it for the benefit of those you meet along the way.

— BARBARA WHITAKER, Independent Executive Senior Sales Director

---

TNT THINKING

To combat the tendency to do nothing, Belsky and Gilovich suggest you change the way you think about things. Here are several of their ideas we've paraphrased in order to help you practice TNT thinking:

- When you're stuck on a decision to do something, think about how you would feel if a proactive step toward what you're considering worked out, but you didn't take the chance. By imagining feelings of regret, you may be able to go beyond your real-life resistance to change.

- When you need to choose between something you currently own and something different or new, imagine yourself in a completely neutral position. Imagine you don't currently own either item or occupy either position, then decide which of the two you would reject rather than which you would select. This eliminates the bias of status quo and the endowment effect. The result is a clearer picture of your options and hopefully less hesitation to act.

- And the ideal way to counter all those paralyzing tendencies is to eliminate the decision process altogether by putting your investments on automatic. Instead of a series of decisions, establish an automatic deduction plan for your retirement account and eliminate the nagging concerns of regret aversion or the endowment effect.

Remember—deciding not to decide is a decision, and doing anything toward investing is better than doing nothing.

The later you start investing, the less risk you can afford to take. The lower the risk, the lower the potential for return.

Six Most Important Things to Do to Begin Now

1. Write the words *"Focus, Commit, Do"* in your journal and vow to follow this cycle over and over again in your financial life.

2. Search for evidence of decision paralysis in your finances.

3. In your journal, write down an example of this paralysis. How long have you been meaning to get around to making a change?

4. Apply the four mindtraps you learned in this chapter to your business. See any ways this new awareness of thinking patterns could benefit your business?

5. If you have your emergency fund in a passbook savings account, find a higher-return option and make a change.

6. When you put down this book today, focus, commit and do at least one thing to benefit your long-term financial security.

Definitions of Living Rich

Giving my husband financial security so he can do
his creative art work.
—*Janis Pereira*

Having a "dream" life. Being stress-free, debt-free,
with total flexibility and a great income.
—*Anne Sullivan*

Having balance and priorities with Mary Kay's philosophies.
—*Kerry DeVilbiss*

Being able to keep my family and faith most important
in life, but still enjoying a successful career.
—*Cecilia James*

Being able to see the big picture in life and looking
forward to the future.
—*Valerie M. Peterson*

A life full of true friends.
—*Silvia Valencia*

No credit-card debt.
—*Jane Jones*

Working without having a boss—I like that very, very much.
—*Josie Abrado*

Changing lives.
—*Andrea Sanders*

Living a Rich Life

Time for the Run

WE'VE COME A LONG WAY TOGETHER IN THIS BOOK, HAVEN'T WE? We've labeled our values and identified our money styles. We've learned how to read the financial news and to understand the basics of investing. We've learned the difference between poverty thinking and rich thinking, poverty words and rich words, and the do's and don'ts of acting rich. We've learned how to balance our time with our priorities, our spending with our values and our investment portfolios with our age and objectives. We've learned how to think long-term to realize major financial goals—free-and-clear home ownership, college educations for our children, millionaire retirement, the fulfillment of our purpose and leaving a legacy our children deserve. We've learned the downright dull details of budgeting, spending less and picking the right insurance plans, fueled by the mindset that when it gets tough, we do it anyway. We've learned how to team up with our husbands, our children and our parents about money. We've learned how to honor the law of the harvest through the giving of our time, our money and our hearts. We've learned how to challenge the "D"mons of debt, divorce and the death of a spouse. And we've learned the cost of procrastination, how to spot the pick-pocketing mindtraps, and how to turn those traps into TNT thinking.

Now it's time to run with what we know and reach for what we want.

I remember a moment many years ago that crystallized in my heart and now speaks so clearly of what we must do. It was a spring afternoon and the breeze was just perfect for an open window in my office. My son Adam, 4 years old at the time, was playing in the side yard with a friend, a little girl with bows in her hair and little lace trimming on the top of her socks.

The giggles caused me to look up from my work and out into the sunshine. Adam was leading the way with the little girl right on his heels. Their little feet were busy and their eyes were full of promise. They were chasing a butterfly. The butterfly must have enjoyed the game because it flew around and around in the yard with its wings almost touching those little wiggly fingers. Those children ran and ran and reached and giggled and the sound was intoxicating. It was light. It was real. It was free. It was full. It was life at its richest.

That's what we must do now—run with a friend, reaching up for a dream, laughing and giggling and loving every step of the way. The financial experts have given us the knowledge; Mary Kay has given us the wisdom. Now we must give it a run, reach for what we want and live the joy of the pursuit. That's the rich life. That's what you deserve. It's waiting. So get your running shoes on and go live it!

END NOTES

CHAPTER ONE

1. Excerpt and illustrations from *The Little Prince* by Antoine de Saint-Exupéry, copyright © 1943 and renewed 1971 by Harcourt, Inc., San Diego, reprinted by permission of the publisher.

2. *A Kick in the Assets: 10 Take-Charge Strategies for Building the Wealth You Want*, by Tod Barnhart, copyright © 1998 by Tod Barnhart. The Berkeley Publishing Group, a division of Penguin Putnam Inc., New York.

3. *Beyond the Relaxation Response*, by Herb Benson. The Berkeley Publishing Group, a division of Penguin Putnam Inc., New York, 1994.

CHAPTER TWO

1. "Buoying Women Investors," by Pam Black. *Business Week*, February 27, 1995.

2. *Six Thinking Hats*, by Edward De Bono, copyright ©1985 by MICA Management Resources, Inc. Little, Brown and Company, Boston, MA.

3. Ibid.

4. Ibid.

5. Reprinted with the permission of Simon & Schuster from *Why Smart People Make Big Money Mistakes*, by Gary Belsky and Thomas Gilovich, copyright © 1999 by Gary Belsky and Thomas Gilovich.

6. Ibid.

7. Used with permission, *Your Complete Guide to Money Happiness*, by Henry S. Brock, copyright © 1997 by Henry S. Brock. Legacy Publishing, Inc., Carson City, NV.

CHAPTER THREE

1. *Keys to Understanding the Financial News*, by Nicholas G. Apostolou and D. Larry Crumbley, copyright ©1989 and 1994 by Barron's Education Series, Inc. Barron's, Hauppauge, NY.

CHAPTER FOUR

1. *10 Steps to Financial Prosperity*, by Bill Griffeth, copyright © 1994 by William C. Griffeth. Warner Books by arrangement with Probus Publishing Company, Chicago.

2. Ibid.

3. Ibid.

4. The Women's Institute for a Secure Retirement, www.wiser.heinz.org.

5. *Your Complete Guide to Money Happiness.*

CHAPTER FIVE

1. *10 Steps to Financial Prosperity.*

2. Ibid.

3. Reprinted with permission from the "1993-94 Annual Survey," copyright © by the College Entrance Examination Board, all rights reserved.

4. National Commission on Retirement Policy, 1998 Report, www.csis.org/retire/facts/html.

5. *The Complete Idiots Guide® to Investing Like a Pro*, by Edward T. Koch and Debra DeSalvo, copyright © 1999 by Ed Koch and Debra DeSalvo. Alpha Books, a division of General Reference, New York.

6. "The Ballpark Estimate" is reprinted with the permission of the American Savings Education Council, www.asec.

CHAPTER SIX

1. *Your Complete Guide to Money Happiness.*

2. *10 Steps to Financial Prosperity.*

3. Ibid.

4. Ibid.

5. *Your Complete Guide to Money Happiness.*

CHAPTER SEVEN

1. *Your Complete Guide to Money Happiness.*

2. "Five Top Money Questions to Ask Before You Get Married," by Jill Gianola, copyright © iVillage. The article appears on the iVillage MoneyLife Channel at www.ivillage.com.

3. "The Finances of Step-Parenting: Six Things Every Family Should Know," by Jill Gianola, copyright © iVillage. The article appears on the iVillage MoneyLife Channel at www.ivillage.com.

4. "His and Hers Retirement," by Ginita Wall, copyright © iVillage. The article appears on iVillage MoneyLife Channel at www.ivillage.com.

5. "Money Harmony: Resolving Money Conflicts in Your Life Relationships," by Olivia Mellan. *MFS Perspectives*, Spring 1999.

6. "The Five Money Mistakes Women in Couples Should Avoid." Women's Institute for a Secure Retirement, www.wise.heinz.org.

7. *10 Steps to Financial Prosperity.*

8. "Smart Credit Strategies for College Students," audiocassette, by Gerri Detweiler. Good Advice Press, Elizaville, NY.

CHAPTER EIGHT

1. *The Wisdom of the Silent Child*, by Marshall Ball, copyright © 1986 by Marshall Stewart Ball. Health Communication, Deerfield Beach, FL.

CHAPTER NINE

1. *Crisis Points: Working Through Personal Problems*, by Julian Sleigh. Anthroposophic Press, Hudson, NY, revised edition 1998.

2. *The Money Book of Personal Finance*, by Richard Eisenberg, copyright ©1996, 1998 by *Money* magazine. Warner Books, New York.

3. "Real Recovery," by Colette Dowling, copyright © iVillage. The article appears on the iVillage MoneyLife Channel at www.ivillage.com.

4. *Making Change*, by Neal Godfrey. Simon & Schuster, New York, 1997.

5. *Ernst & Young's Financial Planning for Women: A Women's Guide to Money for All of Life's Major Events*, copyright © 1999 by Ernst & Young LLP. John Wiley & Sons, Inc., New York.

6. "Divorce Survival Kit: What to Do Now," by Kerry Hannon, copyright © iVillage. The article appears on the iVillage MoneyLife Channel at www.ivillage.com.

CHAPTER TEN

1. *Why Smart People Make Big Money Mistakes.*

INDEX